I0729618

DRAW YOUR OWN
MANTRA

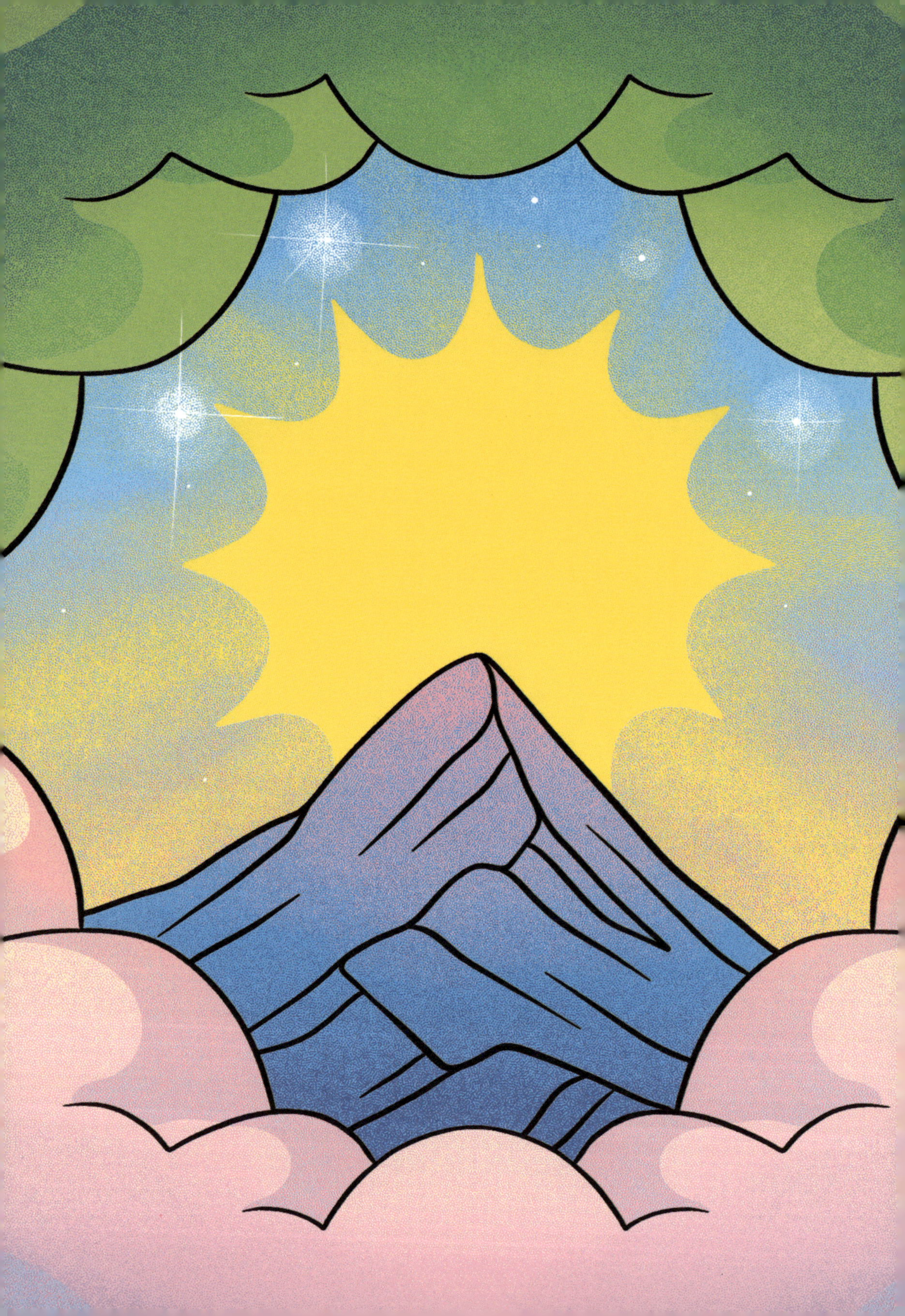

DRAW YOUR OWN MANTRA

CREATE EMPOWERING AFFIRMATION ART

Phe Johnson

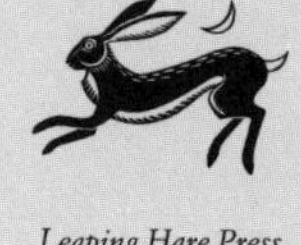

Leaping Hare Press

CONTENTS

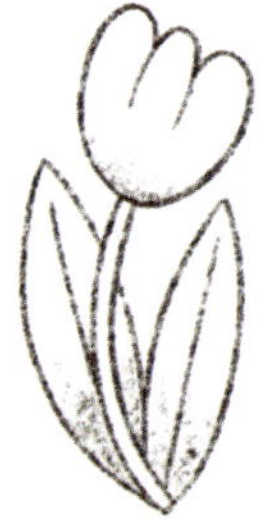

INTRODUCTION

'Over the years, positive messages have become a big feature of my work.'

When I began my illustration journey and was trying to figure out my style, I was mainly drawing nature scenes. I made the mistake of trying to restrict myself in order to produce work of a consistent style, however, this meant that I didn't allow myself much experimentation, which is an incredibly important part of the creative process.

As my illustration style has changed over the years, my methods of producing artwork has changed as well. When I first started illustrating, I was working in watercolour. But as my style changed, I transitioned into producing line drawings, scanning them into Photoshop to add colour to them that way.

I have always preferred to hand-sketch my initial ideas for an illustration, but transitioning to mainly digital work allowed me more scope for experimentation with less equipment.

After a while of scanning and importing drawings into Photoshop, I made the decision to invest in an iPad to allow me to draw digitally. I found that working digitally allowed me to experiment faster, which pushed my style further. I realized that the best thing for me to do creatively was to look for inspiration everywhere, and not just restrict myself to looking for inspiration within the boundaries of whatever style I was working in at that time.

Between the beginning of my illustration career and now, there is so much I have seen and been introduced to that has influenced my work and contributed to the evolution of my illustration style. Keeping my mind open to new ideas keeps me inspired to create, and helps to pull me out of creative blocks.

I now produce a lot of printed products, and positive mantra illustrations have become a huge part of my work that I always enjoy the process of creating. This is an aspect of my artwork that people can really relate to, and through this book, I hope to teach others how to use mantras to evoke certain emotions that they themselves want to be reminded of, and to create pieces to uplift themselves, or share as a gift.

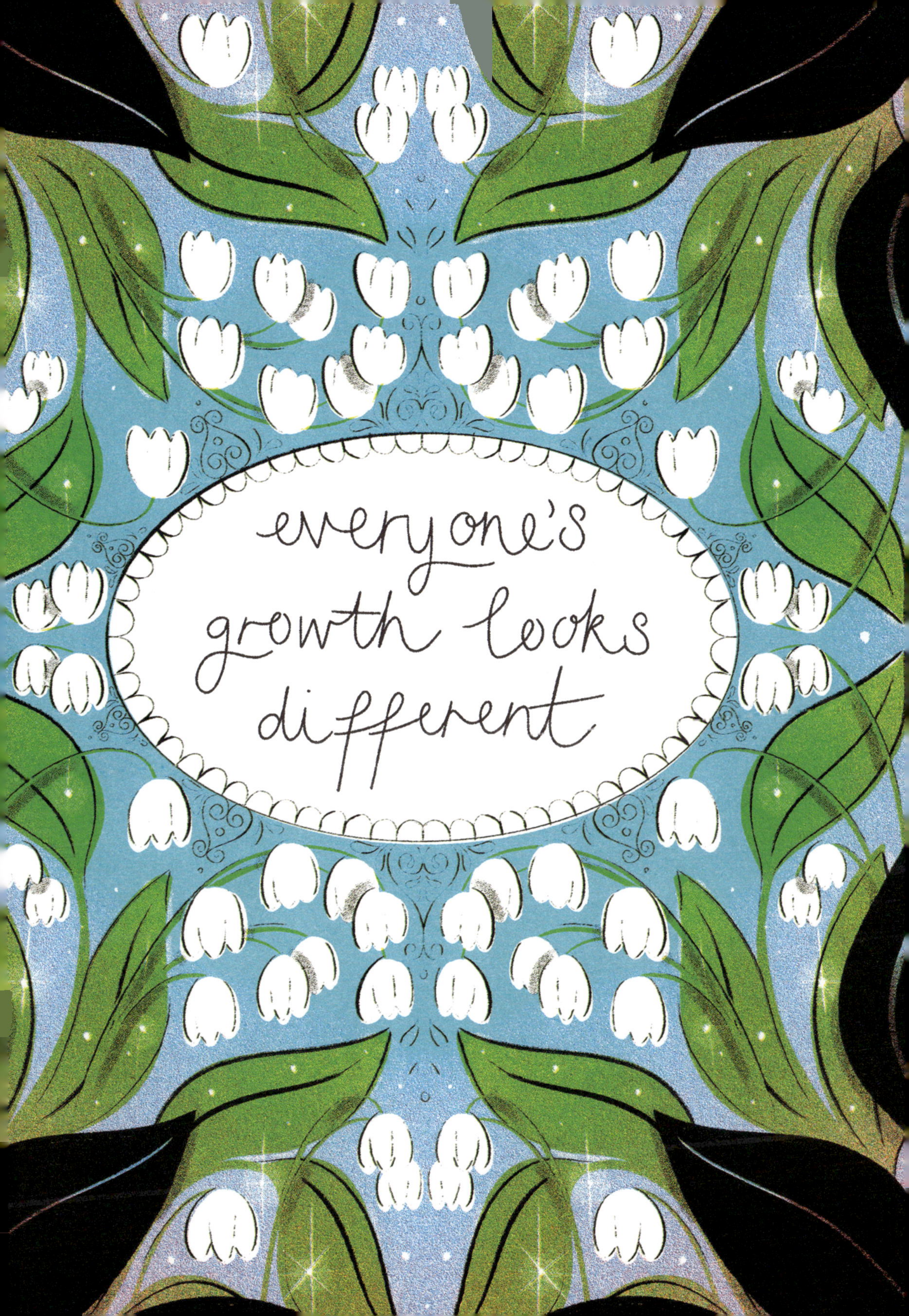

everyone's
growth looks
different

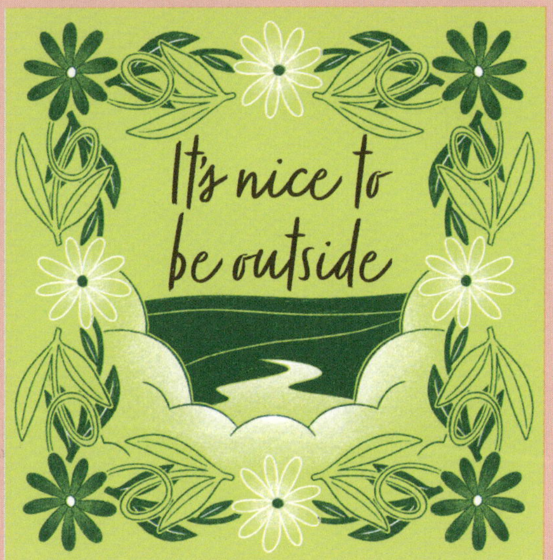
It's nice to be outside

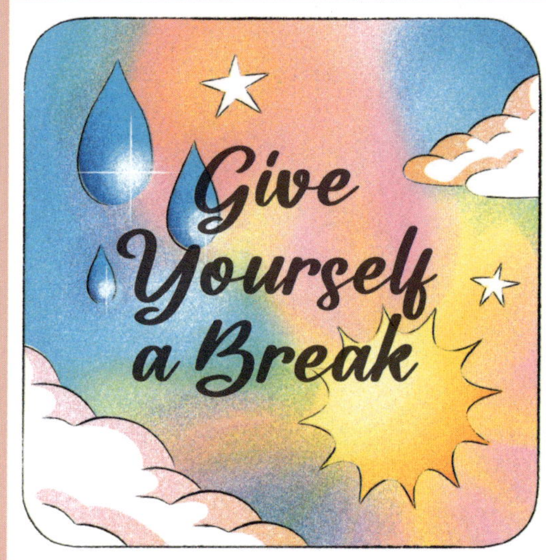
Give Yourself a Break

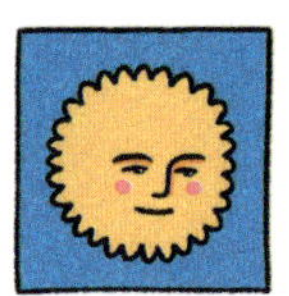
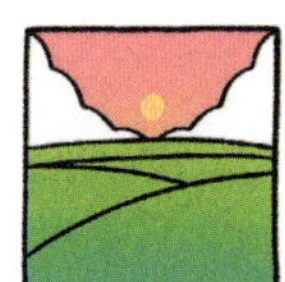
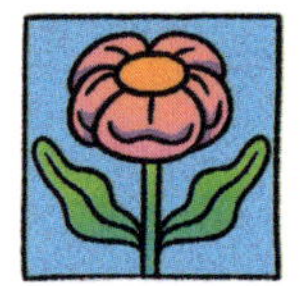
GOOD

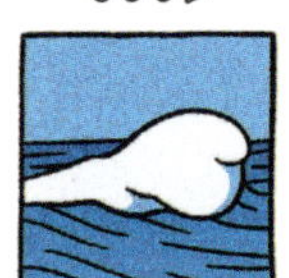

THINGS

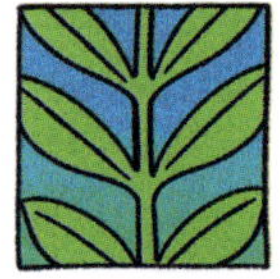
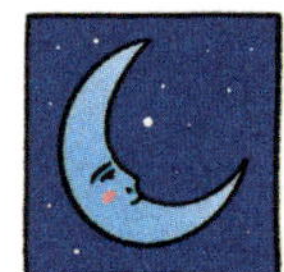
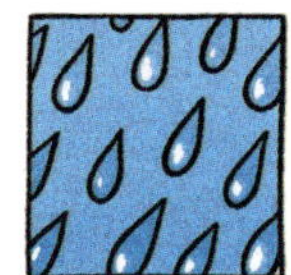
TAKE

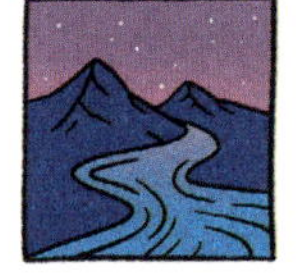
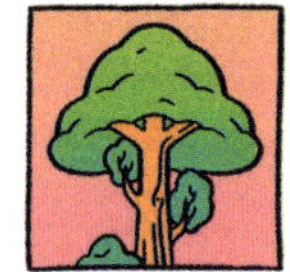
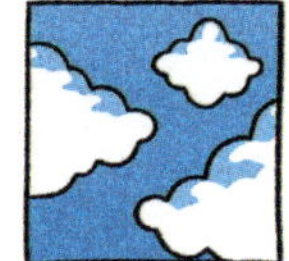
TIME

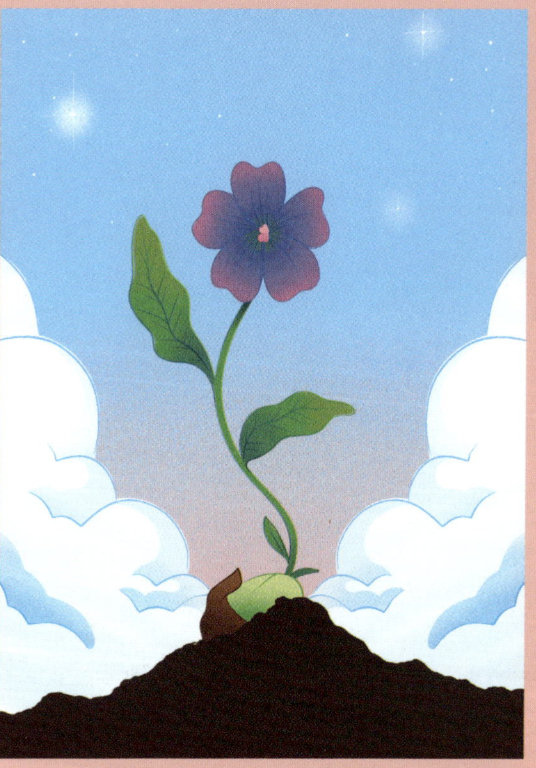

WELCOME

In a world that often focuses on the negative, we are in more need of positive words than ever and, as our lives get busier, the importance of slowing down and taking some time for ourselves only grows.

Nurturing and spending a little time each day focusing on your creativity is just one of many ways that you can introduce a bit of space and mindfulness into your daily life, and this book aims to help you do just that.

Over 12 projects, I will show you how creating your own mantra art can help you to channel your creativity, develop and find your artistic skills and to take a moment for yourself. I will also offer you guidance and inspiration on how to start creating your own art, and equip you with the tools to continue making your own unique mantra art even after you've completed the projects.

I hope you will enjoy this book, and I would love to see your projects. You can find me at:

@phejohnson

phejohnson.com

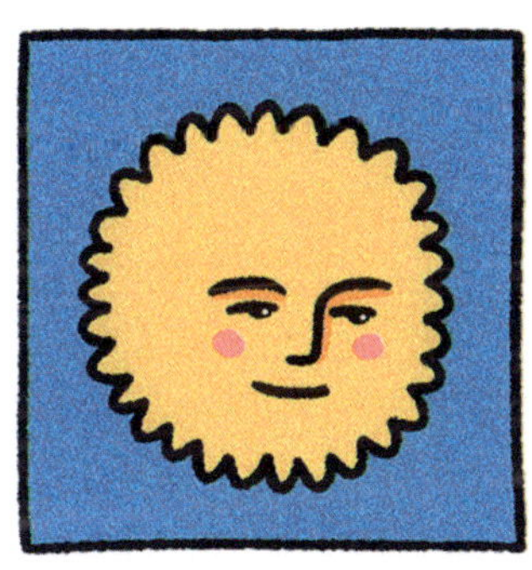 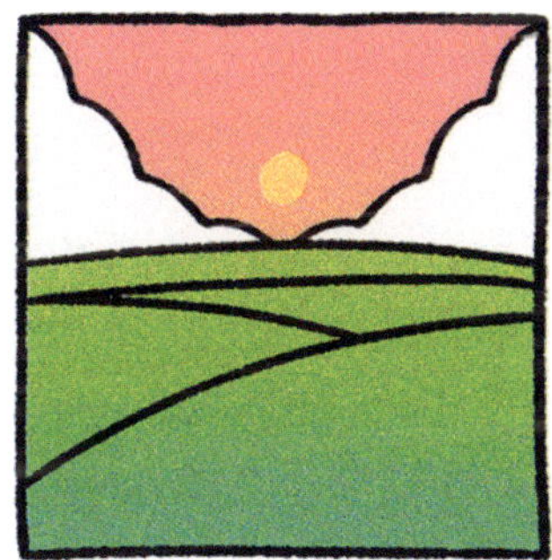 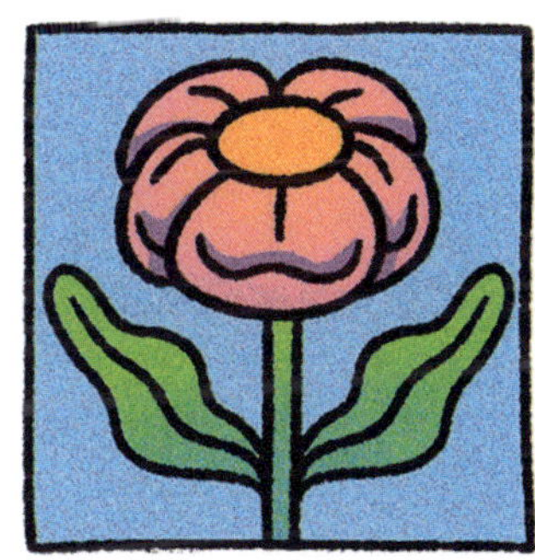

DRAWING YOUR OWN MANTRAS

WHAT IS A MANTRA?

A mantra is defined as a positive phrase or affirmation that you can say to yourself for the purpose of motivation or encouragement. Mantras can be a useful tool to help calm your mind and bring relaxation.

By finding mantras that you connect with, and repeating them to yourself when you need that reassuring message, you will begin to embody them and use them to effect positive change in your life.

WHY DRAW YOUR OWN MANTRA?

There are many benefits to drawing – in addition to releasing your creativity, drawing can help to relieve stress. Completing a piece of artwork that you feel good about is also a great confidence booster. Combining drawing with positive mantras is a great way to improve your mood, creativity and skills, and to create something empowering that you can frame and see every day.

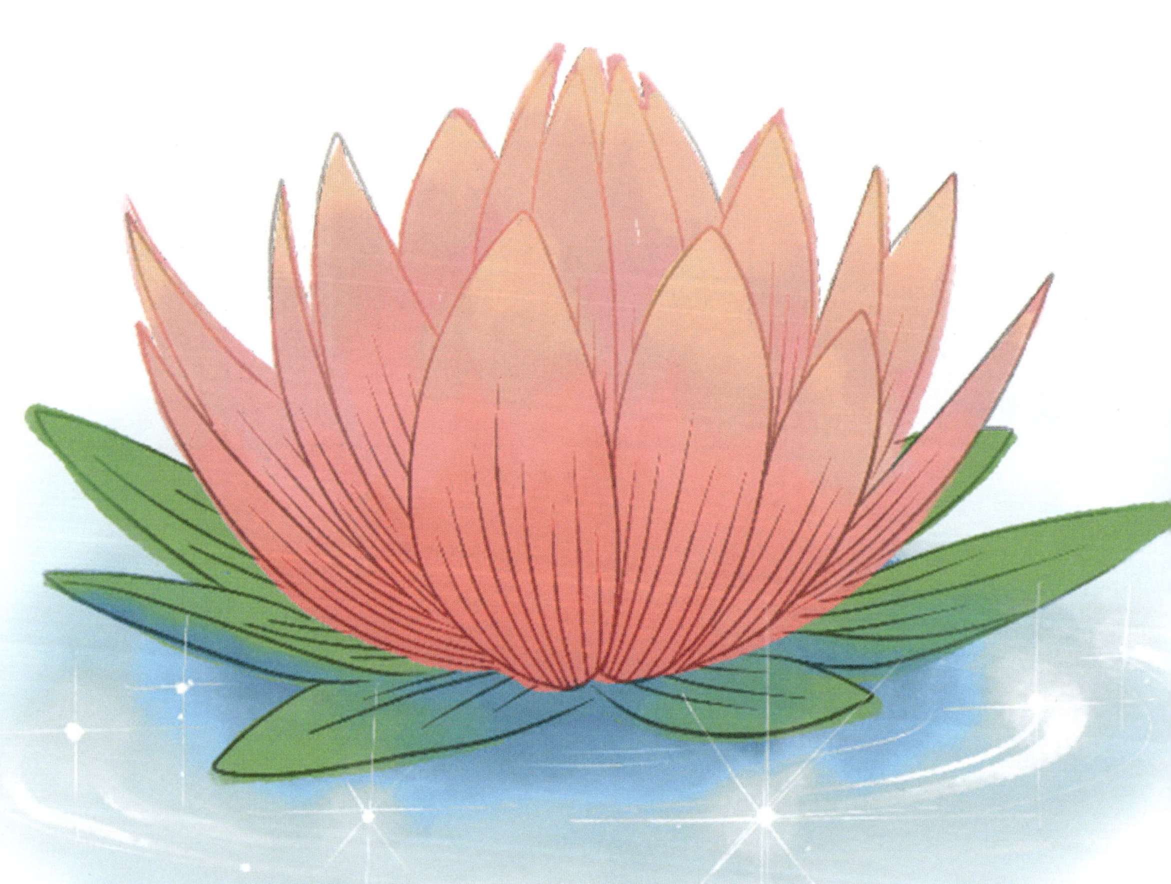

HOW TO USE THIS BOOK

In this book, I will guide you through 12 different mantra projects, leading you through all the aspects you will need to consider before beginning your drawing project, and the step-by-step process for planning and creating your own piece digitally, or using traditional media.

Each project will introduce you to a new artwork technique – from working with symmetry and gradients, to adding texture and colour to your piece – and I will also show you how I created my own piece to help further inspire and guide your choices.

Each mantra has been organized into a specific theme to help you choose a mantra for your specific needs, but you can also choose your project intuitively based on the affirmation. This book is a guide, so please feel free to follow your creativity wherever it leads. If there are certain aspects of the artwork that you would like to change, I encourage you to do so, as this is what will make your artwork personal and unique.

KEY TO THE MANTRAS

CALM
These mantras will help you relax and unwind.

Projects: *Slow Down (see page 49), Take Care of Yourself, (see page 57), Be Kind to Yourself (see page 107), Take a Step Back (see page 131), Progress Not Perfection (see page 139).*

INSPIRE
These mantras will empower and inspire you.

Projects: *Be The Energy You Want to Attract (see page 65), Turn Your Face Towards the Sun (see page 75), I Believe in Myself (see page 123), Progress Not Perfection (see page 139).*

UPLIFT
These mantras will help boost your mood.

Projects: *You're Doing Great (see page 83), Better Days Ahead (see page 91), Keep Your Head Up (see page 99), This Too Shall Pass (see page 115).*

WHO IS THIS BOOK FOR?

Whether you're new to drawing, have a little experience or have a lifetime of experience, this book can be for you. Spending as little as ten minutes a day on these projects will help you feel the holistic benefits of drawing, and all you need in order to participate is your own creativity, and a pen and paper. No previous experience is required!

DIGITAL VS HAND DRAWING

You will see that in the examples for each exercise, I have also provided alternative instructions for different medias that you can use to hand draw your piece, which will be just as effective.

If you would like to draw digitally but are new to this type of drawing, I have included a brief guide to the basic tools in Photoshop that you can use for these projects. If you would like to work digitally using different software, please feel free to do so, as the techniques I will be guiding you through can be applied to all mediums.

GETTING STARTED

Before you dive in to drawing your own affirmation art, there are some important things to consider. In this section, I will guide you through these basic preparations you can make to get ready for your project, both artistically and emotionally.

Spending time carefully considering the choices over the following pages will not only help you build your excitement and ideas for your project, but will ensure you have a really solid groundwork to create your artwork on, making for a more enjoyable creative process and a higher quality piece further down the line.

So, take a few calming breaths, clear your mind and prepare to draw your own mantra!

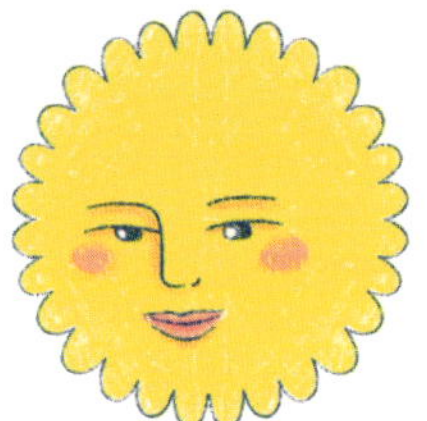

WHAT YOU'LL NEED

For the drawing exercises in this book, I will give you various media options to choose from, but if not all of these tools are available to you, don't worry! Great artwork can be created with just a pencil and a piece of paper.

You will need a sketchbook, and I also recommended that you have a notebook of some kind to jot down your ideas, as this will be helpful during the planning stages of your illustrations, and will be a very valuable tool to refer back to for inspiration.

Here is a list of tools you can choose from for this book:

☆ Pencil or pen
☆ Sketchbook
☆ Notebook
☆ Coloured pencils
☆ Watercolour paint
☆ Graphic markers
☆ Fine liners
☆ Artist crayons
☆ Digital drawing equipment and software

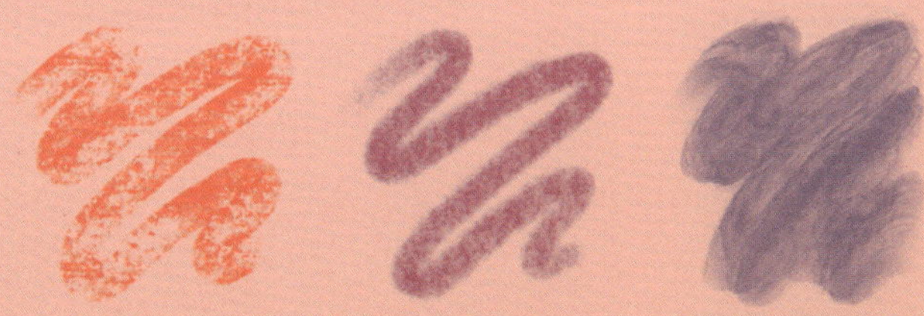

trust the process

CHOOSE YOUR MANTRA

This first stage of your project is just as important as choosing your media, and is a decision that will help guide all of your stylistic choices. It's time to select your mantra!

You want your mantra to be something that will inspire you or the person you are creating your piece for, so take the time to find the right words, and don't be afraid to alter them until you feel they are right.

If you are feeling unsure about what mantra to choose, it can be helpful to jot down your ideas in a notebook to revisit after a break, or to play around with different variations of your ideas.

Some questions you can ask yourself when developing or choosing your mantra are:

☆ What positive words do I need to hear right now?

☆ What are my goals, and what words can help empower me on my way to achieving them?

☆ What advice would I give to a friend in a similar situation?

☆ What words fill me with joy or hope when I hear them?

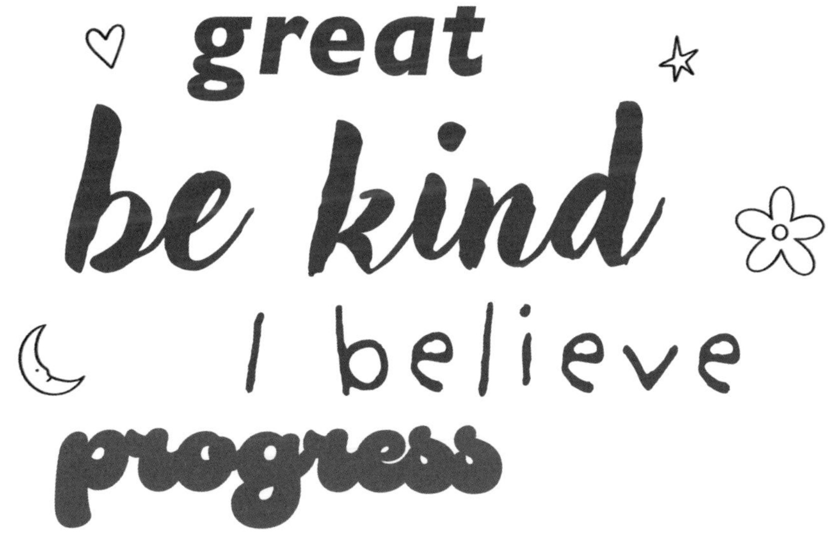

USING PHOTOSHOP

Whether you would like to try drawing a mantra completely digitally, or want to experiment with mixing digital and traditional methods, learning a few basic techniques of digital drawing will give you the building blocks to get started. I have used Photoshop to create the illustrations within this book, so on the following pages, I have included a guide to the essential Photoshop skills you will need. You can also use Illustrator or the Procreate app on the iPad if you choose.

SETTING UP YOUR CANVAS

Your canvas is the area on your screen in Photoshop where you will create your artwork. You have the ability in Photoshop to make your canvas any size you wish, so if you have a picture frame and would like to make a piece of artwork to fit in it, you can input the exact measurements you need. However, there are also preset sizes. If you are drawing your artwork for print, I would recommend using one of the standard paper sizes that you can find in the 'Print' section (for example, A4 or A5).

1. Open Photoshop and go to 'File → New'. To use a preset size, simply click on the preset and move on to the instructions in Step 4. To create your own custom-sized canvas, open 'New Document' on the right-hand-side of the window. You will see two boxes where you can type in the width and height that you would like.

2. Click on the 'Resolution' section. Input the number of dots per inch you want your artwork to have.

3. Click on the 'Colour Mode' section. Select the colour mode you would like to use. Click 'Create' to finish setting up your canvas.

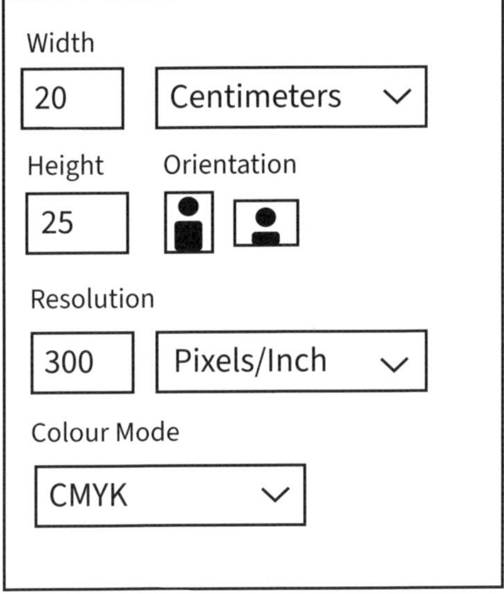

4. When you have created your document, find the layers panel on the right-hand side of the screen. Here you will see your background, which will be set as default white. This layer will also be locked. To unlock this layer and edit your background colour, select your background layer and click on the lock icon. Once your background layer is unlocked, you can change the colour by clicking on the 'Colour' tab at the top of the right-hand panel. Choose your colour, click on the 'Paint Bucket' tool on the left-hand panel, and click on your canvas to fill it with colour.

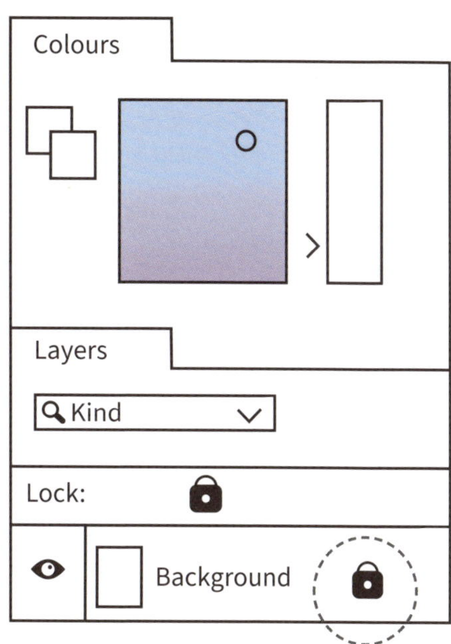

Explaining DPI

DPI (which means 'dots per inch') refers to the amount of ink dots that will be printed per inch when you print an image. The higher DPI your image has (or the more dots per inch), the more detail you will be able to capture in your print, and the clearer your image will be.

The minimum resolution you should use for anything you intend to print is 300 DPI, as this will give you a nice, sharp image quality when it comes to printing. Another common resolution you may see is 72 DPI.

This is a low resolution, but is common for web images and other digital applications.

RGB (meaning 'red-green-blue') is the setting you should choose if you are making images that will only be shared digitally. CMYK (meaning 'cyan-magenta-yellow-black') is the setting you should choose if you will be printing your images, as this setting matches the inks most printers use.

USING LAYERS

Layers in Photoshop are a great tool if you are adding multiple elements to your canvas. Image layers are like transparent sheets stacked on top of each other, which means you can see through each layer to the one below, and organize your images so that certain images sit on top of or beneath others. I would recommend creating a new layer for each aspect of your artwork, as this will be very helpful if you want to make any adjustments to individual elements down the line.

1. To create a new layer, click on the icon in the bottom right-hand-corner of the screen that looks like a sheet of paper with the corner folded.

2. If you would like to re-order your layers, simply click on your layer, then hold down and drag it to the position you would like to move it to.

3. To delete a layer, click on the layer you would like to delete and press the backspace button to delete it.

ADJUSTING LAYER TYPES

The standard setting for each new layer is 'Normal', which will give your layers the appearance of being stacked on top of each other. However, another layer type that I like to use a lot in my artwork is 'Multiply'. This layer type is really useful if you want to experiment with colour; if you place two different colours on your canvas slightly overlapping and change their layer types to 'Multiply', you will see that the colours will blend together where they overlap. The best way to learn about the different layer types is to experiment, so get some colours on your canvas and get experimenting!

1. If you would like to change your layer type, click on the drop-down menu that will be set to the default 'Normal' setting. This will show you all of the options you can use to change your layer type. You will see the 'Multiply' option as the fourth option in the list.

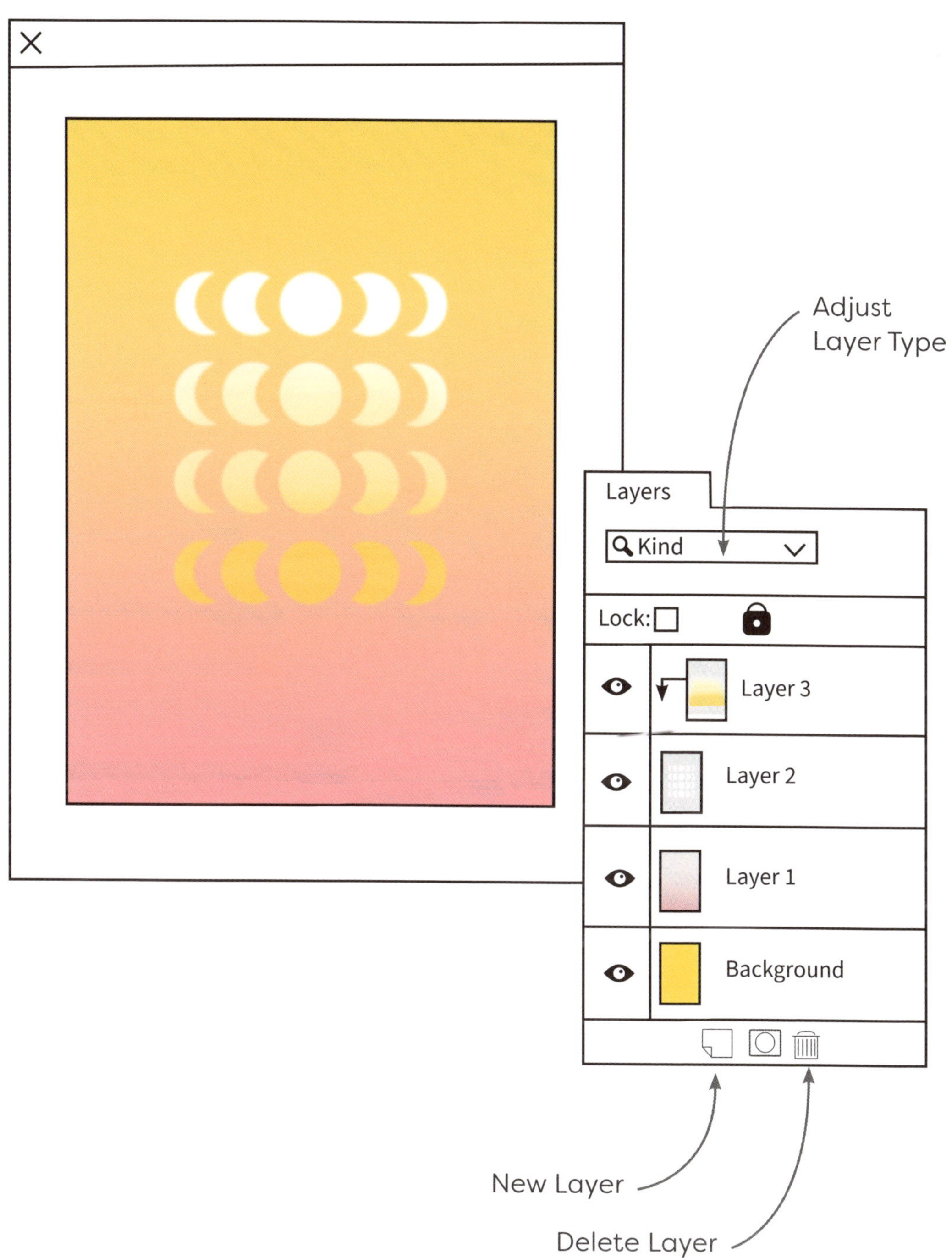

Adjust
Layer Type
Layers
Kind
Lock:
Layer 3
Layer 2
Layer 1
Background
New Layer
Delete Layer

SELECTING PENS AND COLOURS

The 'Brush' and 'Colour' tools are the most important tools you will need when working on any illustrative elements in your piece. These are the tools you will use to make your marks on the canvas, and many of the brushes mimic real-life mediums such as pen, pencil, pastel and paint. The colour tool will also give you access to over 16 million colours.

1. To select your brush, click on the 'Brush' tool on the left-hand side of your screen. The standard brush preset will give you a clean line, however, if you open the brush preset picker and scroll down, you will see that there are many different brush presets that you can experiment with to create different effects. Once you have selected your brush, select the colour you want to use from the 'Colour' panel, which you can find on the right-hand side of your screen.

MOVING AND RESIZING ILLUSTRATIONS

Something you may need to do throughout your drawing process is to 'transform' parts of your drawing by moving, resizing, rotating or reflecting.

1. To move your object, use the 'Move' tool (which is the first tool in the left-hand toolbar), and click and drag your object where you would like it to go.

2. To resize your object, click on the 'Move' tool, and hover your cursor over one of the corners of your object until the diagonal arrow appears. Once this arrow has appeared, click and drag inwards to make your object smaller, or outwards to make it bigger. If you would like to maintain the proportions of your object, hold down the 'Shift' key on your keyboard while you are clicking and dragging.

3. To rotate your object, click on the 'Move' tool, and hover your cursor about 5mm (¼in) away from the corner of your object until the curved arrow appears. Once this arrow has appeared, you can click and drag left and right to rotate your object. If you would like to rotate your image by more definite amounts, you can go to 'Edit' on the toolbar right at the top of the screen, then go down the list to 'Transform', where you can find more options to rotate your object. You will also find the option to flip your object vertically or horizontally in this same panel.

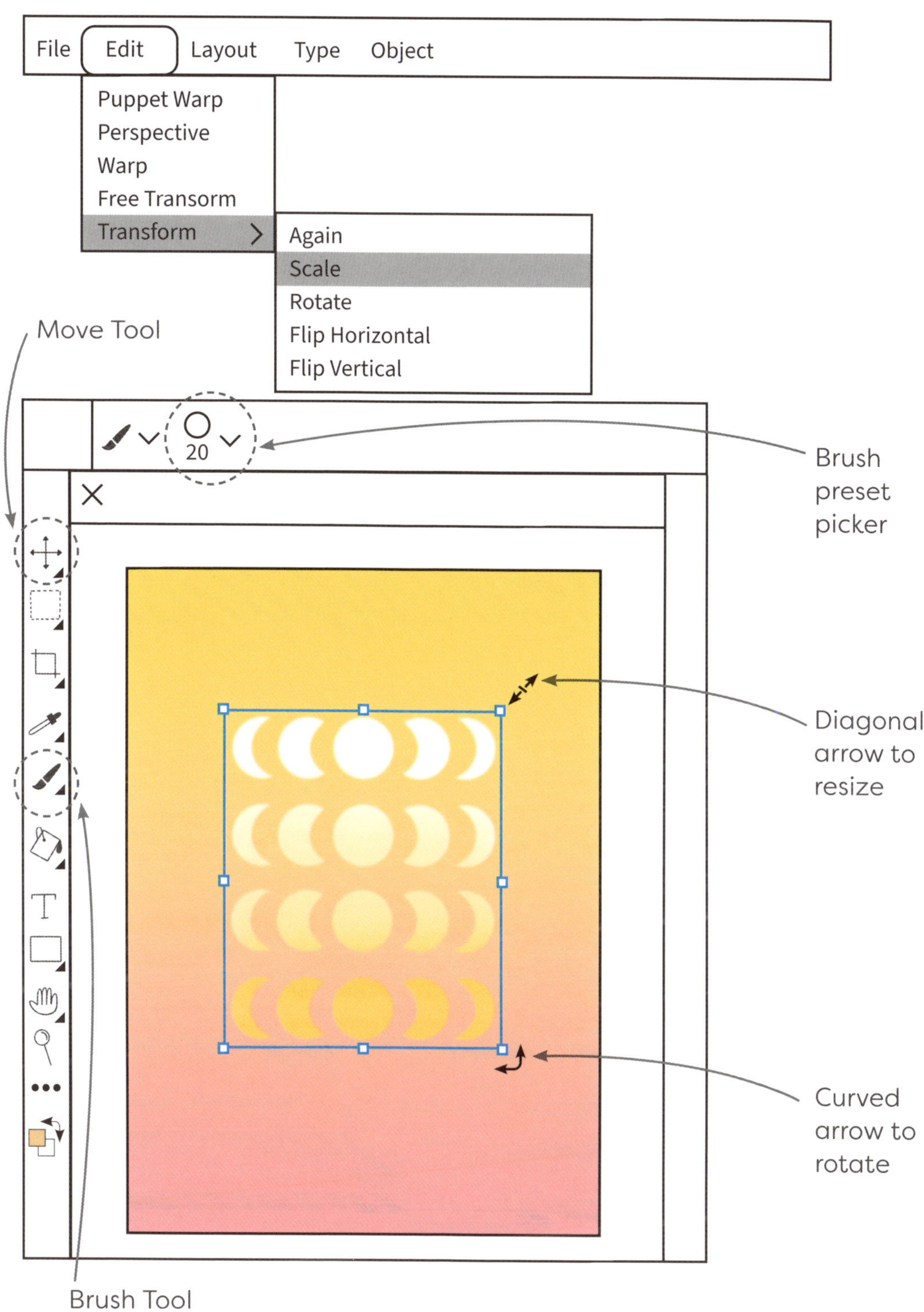

File
Edit
Layout
Type
Object
Puppet Warp
Perspective
Warp
Free Transorm
Transform
Again
Scale
Rotate
Flip Horizontal
Flip Vertical
Move Tool
20
Brush preset picker
Diagonal arrow to resize
Curved arrow to rotate
Brush Tool

ADDING TEXT

You can add text to your canvas by using the 'Type' tool near the bottom of the left-hand toolbar. Once you click on this icon, you will see options appear on the top toolbar that will allow you to edit your font, which will help you select and add the perfect mantra to your piece.

1. To add text to your canvas, click on the 'Type' tool on the left-hand toolbar, and then click on your canvas.

2. To choose a font, click on the 'Font' selector on the horizontal panel to the top left of your canvas. This will open up a drop-down menu with a list of all the fonts that are installed on your program. You can easily change fonts by clicking on the one you would like to use.

3. To choose your font size, you can increase or decrease the size by changing the number by 'pt' in the 'Size' box just along from the 'Font' selector.

ADJUSTING TEXT

A simple way that you can get creative with your lettering is by changing the size of your text, as well as the amount of space between the letters (tracking), and the space between the lines (leading). You can find these controls in the 'Properties' panel once you've added some text to your canvas.

1. To access the 'Properties' panel, go to 'Window → Properties'.

2. To adjust your tracking, select one of the numbered options that appears in the drop-down menu when you click on the down arrow, or type a specific number into the window if there is a specific amount of spacing that you would like to use for your tracking. Positive numbers will increase the spaces between the letters, and negative numbers will reduce the spacing between the letters.

3. To adjust your leading, select one of the numbered options that appears in the drop-down menu when you click on the down arrow, or type a specific number into the window if there is a specific amount of spacing that you would like to use for your leading.

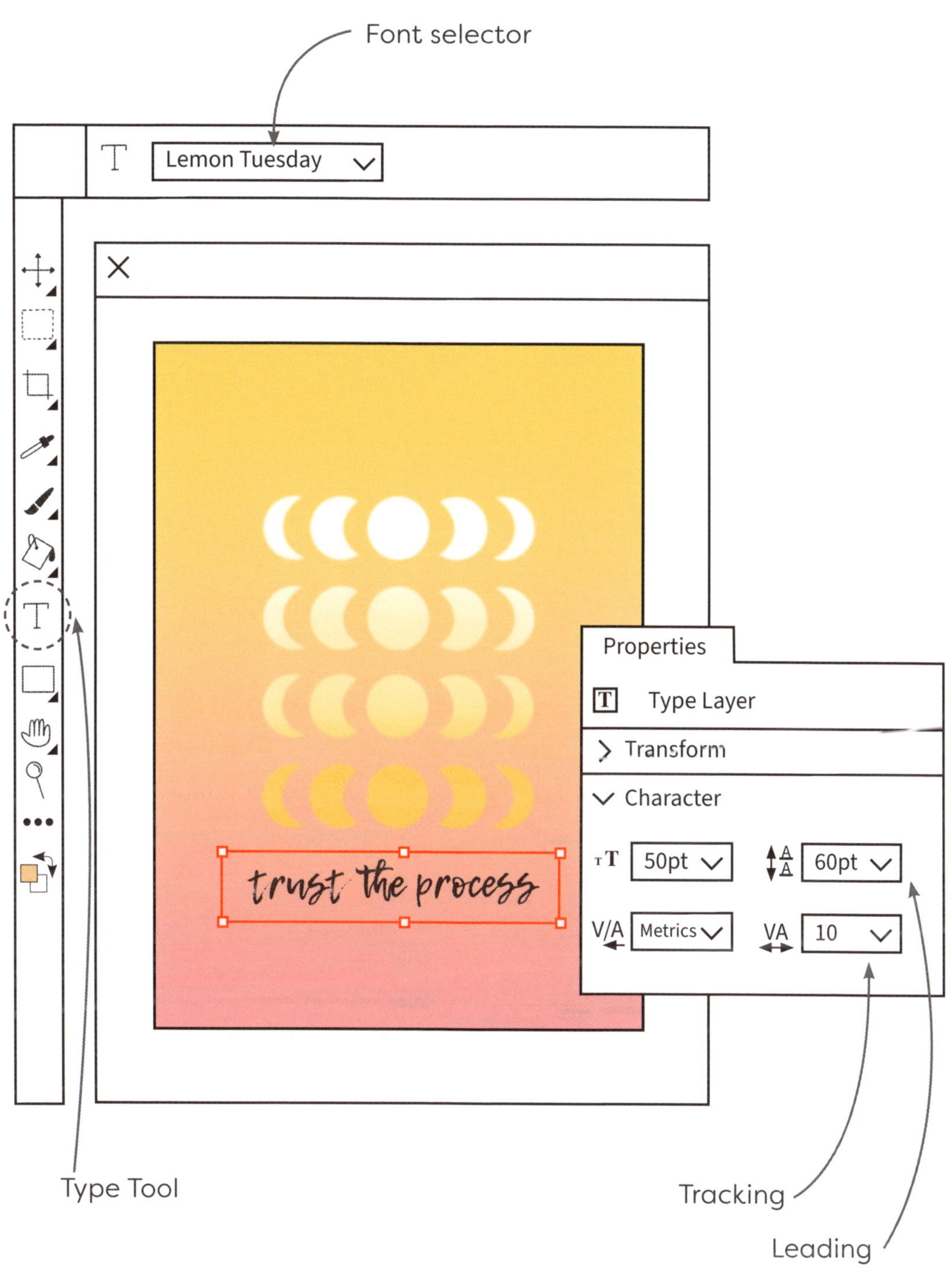
Font selector
Lemon Tuesday
Properties
Type Layer
Transform
Character
50pt
60pt
Metrics
10
trust the process
Type Tool
Tracking
Leading

CHOOSE YOUR COLOUR PALETTE

The colours you chose to use in your illustration play an important role in influencing the mood of your piece. Everyone is different, so take some time when planning your mantra drawings to consider what emotions you want to evoke, and test out some different colour palettes, paying attention to what emotions you feel when looking at certain colours.

Brighter colours such as red, orange or yellow may make you feel more energized and motivated.

Cooler and more muted colours such as blues and purples may make you feel more relaxed and calm.

Some questions you can ask yourself when developing and choosing your colour palette are:

☆ How do these colours make me feel?

☆ Which colours make me feel calm?

☆ Which colours make me feel motivated?

☆ Which colours make me feel happy?

Visualization Exercise to Inspire Creative Ideas

If you find yourself feeling uninspired or creatively stuck, try this visualization exercise to remove creative blocks, and get your artistic ideas flowing again.

Find a comfortable seated or standing position where you won't be disturbed, and close your eyes. You may like to keep a paper and pen nearby to note down your findings.

Focus on your breath, taking slow, steady inhales, and quiet your mind.

When you feel settled, imagine that there is a large blank page of paper in front you, with a beautiful fountain pen resting next to it.

Pick up the pen and hold it in your hand. Then, as quickly as you can, imagine flicking the pen vigorously towards the piece of paper, splattering ink all over it. Try not to put too much thought into this action, and allow the first colour, image and shape that comes to mind to form on the paper.

Continue to flick the pen and pay attention to what is created on the page. The colours and shapes may change, and it's worth paying attention to them all.

Practise this exercise for a few minutes, and then write down any ideas or observations you made during the visualization.

CHOOSE YOUR MEDIA

The type of media you use in your illustration is another important tool you can use to evoke a particular emotion in your piece, and the way your media looks on the page and how it feels to use are key factors to consider when deciding on your media.

Using something like watercolour paint may be a more relaxing process, as the colours go on the page more delicately, and watching the paint spreading through the water as you are applying it can be a very calming experience. In contrast to this, using something like a marker pen will give an instant and bold colour application that you might need to feel more confident in before applying it to the page.

These media swatches will give you an idea of just some of the types of media you could choose from:

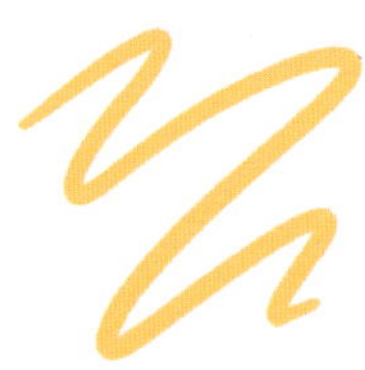

MARKERS

Because these are quick-drying, they make a great choice for when you want to apply bold colour quickly and easily without making a mess. I love to use them when I want a smooth finish to my lines, and they are also available in a variety of sizes, which make them suitable for many uses.

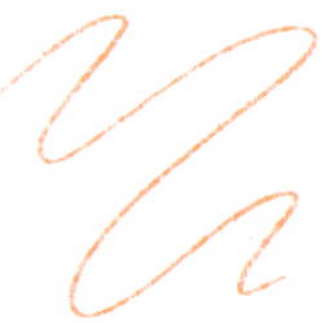

PENCILS

These are a versatile media, as you can use minimal colours to produce simpler drawings, or take your time with layering colours to create hyper-realistic artworks. They are a great choice if you want to have more control over where your colour goes, and the amount of detail you are adding into your work.

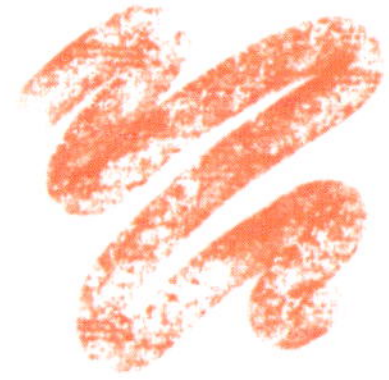

CRAYONS

Like markers, crayons are a great choice when you want a quick colour application without mess. They are available in a range of colours, and are a good option for artists looking to experiment. The waxy texture of crayons also creates unique effects on the page that can't be achieved with other types of media.

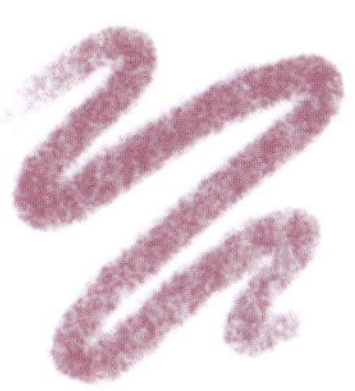

CHALK

The soft texture of chalk provides a great option for when you want a lighter colour application on the page. You can create different effects depending whether you use the sharper edge, for more defined lines, or the flat edge, for shading.

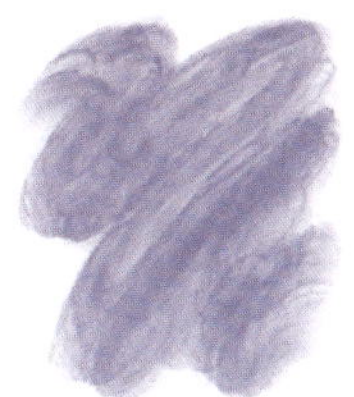

WATERCOLOUR PAINTS

These water-based paints have a translucent quality when applied to paper. They are easily mixed together with water to create a variety of shades and hues.

ACRYLIC PAINTS

Acrylic paints are versatile, quick-drying, and can be used on many surfaces. They have a strong colour application and can be applied in thin layers, or thick, depending on the desired finish.

Free Drawing Exercise for Joy and Play

When testing out your different medium types, try this free drawing exercise to help you get to know your tools better, and have fun playing around with doodles and ideas that you can use later.

1. Take a blank sheet of paper or a notebook, and gather as many different forms of media as you can.

2. Taking one form of media at a time, draw a selection of faces and expressions. These faces can be as detailed or as simple as you like – just have fun and draw as wide a range of expressions and emotions as you can.

3. One at a time, experiment with each different media, and pay attention to anything you like or observe about it.
For example, you may find that watercolour evokes sadness and calm more effectively than crayon and chalk, which may be better for more playful and cheerful emotions. You may also like to experiment using more than one media for each face, to see how the two combinations work together.

4. Save the drawings from this activity for future reference when you would like help choosing the right media for a project.

CHOOSE YOUR LETTERING

Choosing the right lettering to complement your illustration is a great way to bring your artwork together. Try your own handwriting, do research, use different digital fonts and experiment with cases and text size to create the right impact for your artwork.

You may feel drawn to a particular style of lettering at first glance, but you may want to experiment with some different options before deciding which one works best with your artwork and also suits the tone of your mantra message.

Below are some examples of different types of lettering that you may want to use in your mantra artworks.

HANDWRITING IN CAPITALS

handwriting in lower case

calligraphy script

BLOCK CAPITALS

OUTLINE LETTERS

Here, you can see an example mantra 'slow down', written using these different styles. Which one do you think best suits the mantra message, and why? Do you think the different lettering evokes different emotions from the mantra message?

Take some time to practise some lettering styles that you might like to use in your mantra illustration, and think about which styles of lettering would suit different types of mantras.

SLOW DOWN

slow down

slow down

SLOW DOWN

SLOW DOWN

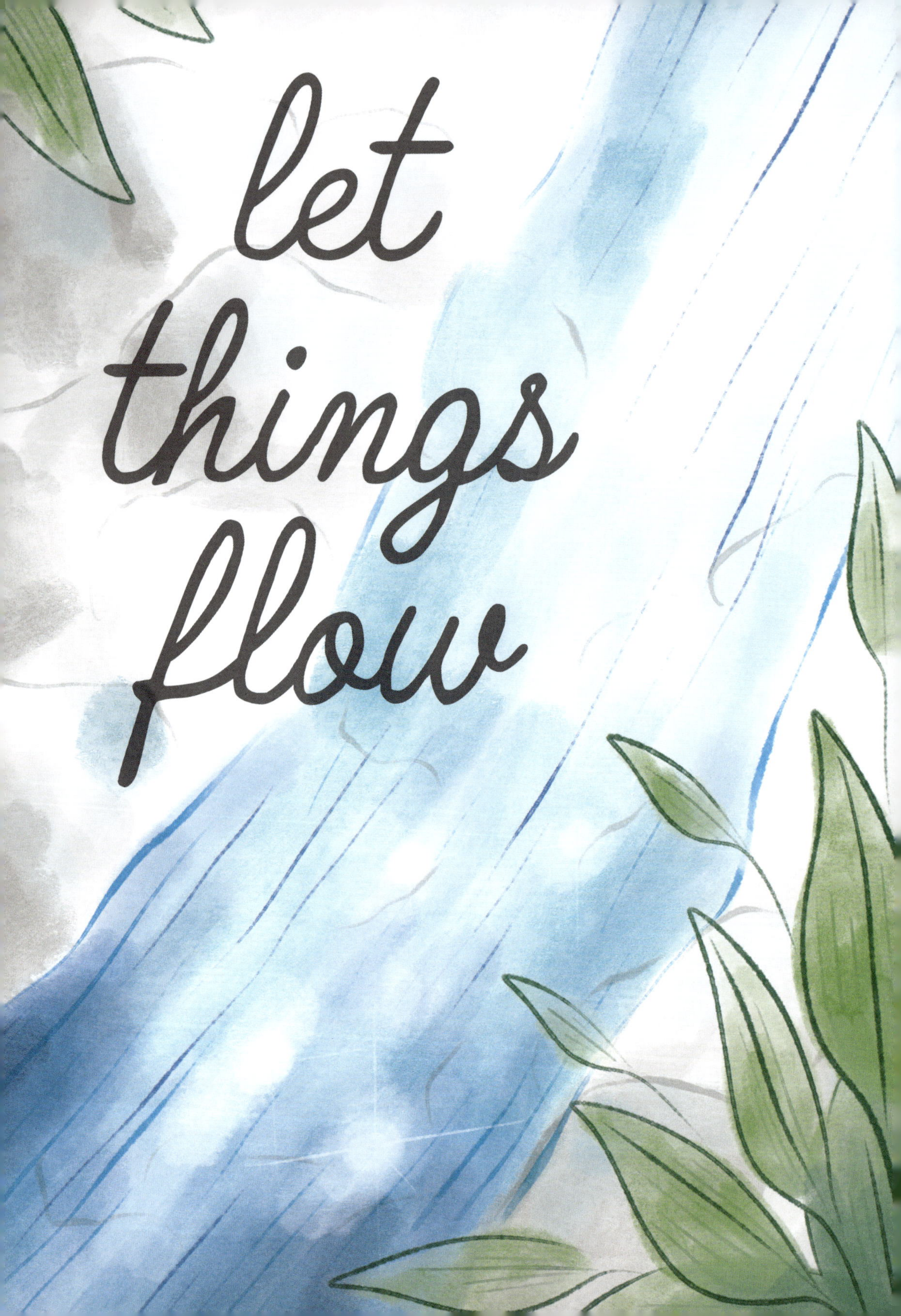

let
things
flow

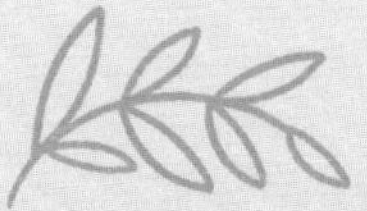

FIND YOUR INSPIRATION AND STYLE

In this section, we will go through some simple exercises to help develop your own unique style. Finding your inspiration and art style is a challenging but rewarding journey, and one of the many holistic benefits of drawing is that it helps you to connect with yourself, to explore how you're feeling and what you like. In fact, the best part of creating something is often the *process* of creating it. The next pages will help guide you through your own creative process, while remaining playful. You don't need to confine yourself to one style – you can have fun exploring and learning about every unique side of your style and self! This is the most important part.

Finding your artistic and creative style can be a long process of researching and experimenting, as there is so much inspiration out there. A good place to start when looking to develop your own style and pieces is to spend some time thinking about what kinds of artwork you naturally gravitate towards, and what interests and inspires you.

- ☆ Do you gravitate towards minimalistic or more complex pieces?
- ☆ Do you like a lot of colour?
- ☆ Do you prefer more abstract or more realistic pieces of art?
- ☆ Why do you think you are drawn to particular styles of artwork?

WHAT ARE YOU INSPIRED BY?

It is also helpful to consider what inspires you in your daily life and dreams.

For example, I draw a lot of inspiration from the illustration and design styles I had when I was a child. Finding the things that inspire you creatively is hugely beneficial.

Your inspirations are an important part of what makes you unique, and learning what these things are can be a hugely rewarding way to discover more about yourself.

Consider the following questions, and think about how you could reflect the answers in your art through medium, colour, lettering and illustration.

☆ What inspires me in life?

☆ What brings me peace?

☆ What makes me feel powerful?

☆ What colours or objects bring me joy?

☆ Which feelings and emotions do I feel most strongly?

☆ What do my favourite objects say about me and how do they represent me (for example, what does my favourite outfit say about me)?

☆ What characteristics am I most proud of in myself?

Sensory Hunt to Help You Find Your Inspiration

The next time you find yourself creatively stuck, spend five minutes outside and try to notice the sounds, smells and textures around you. Focus on being as present and engaged as you can, and jot down any observations or ideas that may come to mind in a notebook, or take some photos to refer to later.

Whether you are surrounded by trees, the sea or a cityscape, there is a lot of inspiration to be gathered from your surroundings, and you never know where inspiration will come from.

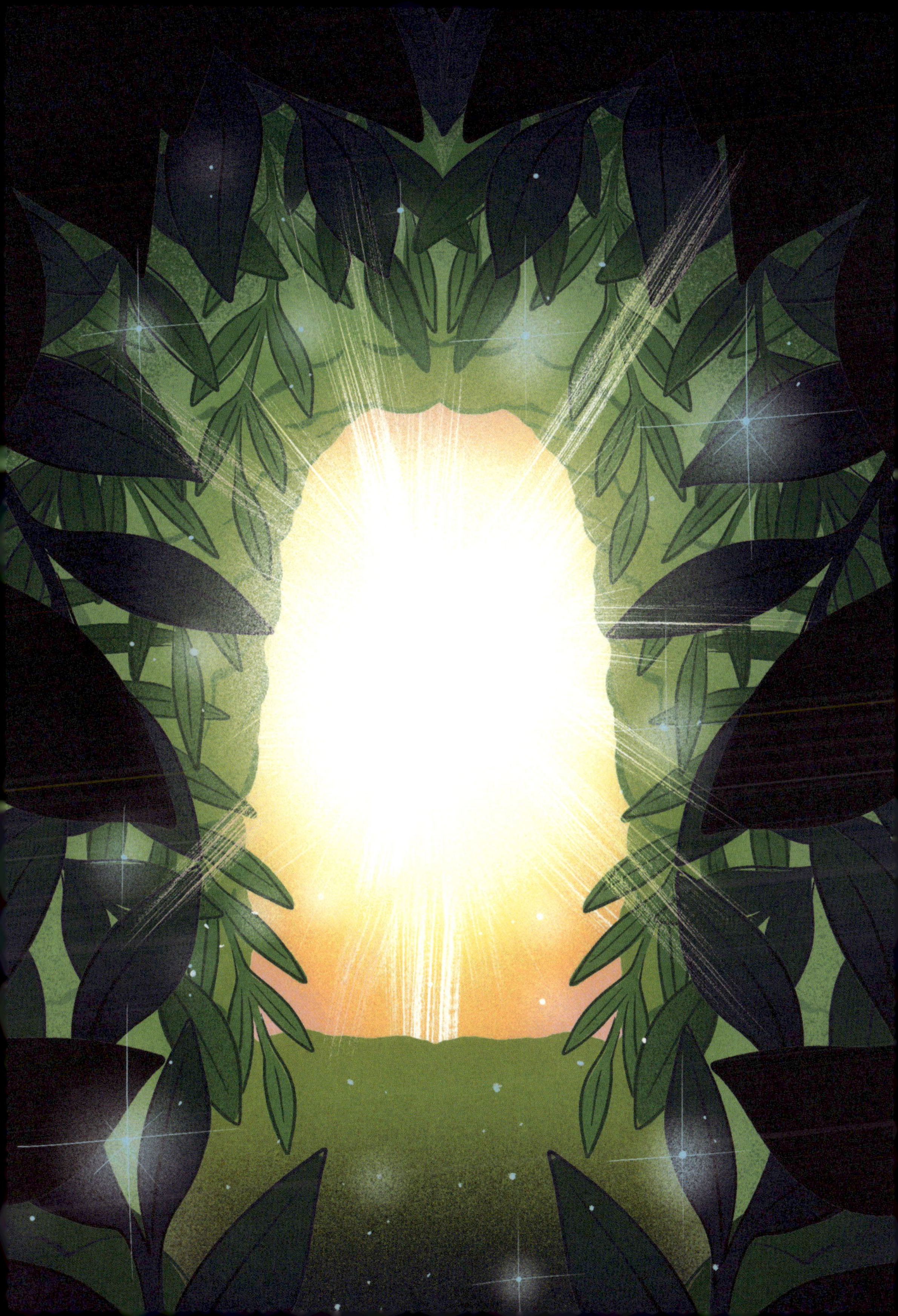

HOW TO PREPARE A MOOD BOARD

Mood boards are a great way to gather all of your ideas and inspirations together before beginning a project, and can act as a great visual aid to help you when you're creating your piece. You never know when inspiration may strike, and it's always a good idea to try and take pictures of anything you may see in your day-to-day life that sparks creativity to add to your mood boards. You can also make a note of things that inspire you to return to later so that you don't lose that spark of inspiration!

Creating a mood board is a simple process, and is something you can create digitally, or traditionally. You can use a glue stick and magazines to create a collage mood board, print off images that inspire you and place them on a piece of paper, or create a digital document with all of your images on it. The method is up to you.

Here is an example of a mood board I created when I was developing an idea for a calming mantra.

I began my mood board by taking a minute to see what came to mind when I thought of the word 'calming'. I pictured forests, sunsets and the sea, so I researched inspiring photos of these to include on my mood board.

You can either use your own images on your mood board, or you can research other images that inspire you. Just make sure that you don't mimic these images too closely in your final piece (especially if you are including another artist's work on your mood board); if the images are quite similar, be sure you have permission to use them.

Once I had picked out some artwork and images that I found relaxing to look at, I created a palette inspired by all of these aspects to tie everything together.

I also included the type of lettering and media I thought would suit this piece, so that everything that I might need to refer back to while drawing my mantra illustration was in one place and easy to reference.

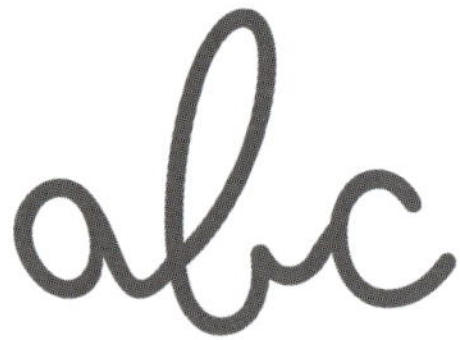

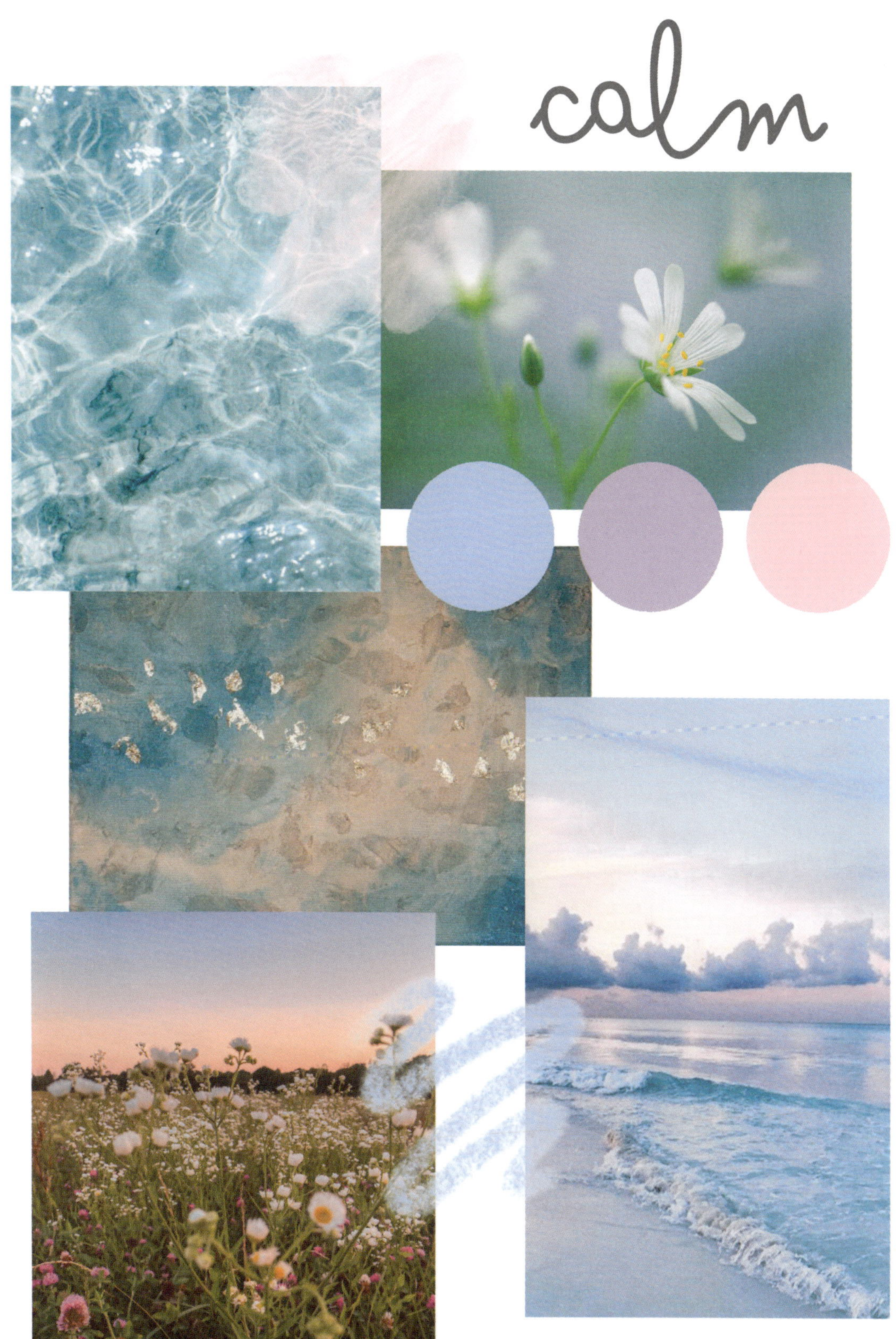

calm

USING DIFFERENT DRAWING TECHNIQUES

Experimenting with different drawing techniques is a really valuable way to find your artistic voice. Many artists have a distinct style, and you may feel the pressure to do the same and narrow down the variation in your style. But you can gain so much artistically through pushing the boundaries and trying things you may not have thought suited you.

Throughout each project, I will teach you a range of techniques to help you develop your style, and I encourage you to try different techniques for the mantras alongside the ones suggested. You may even like to create two different versions of the same mantra using different techniques, observing the effects this has on the piece, and how it alters the mood it conveys.

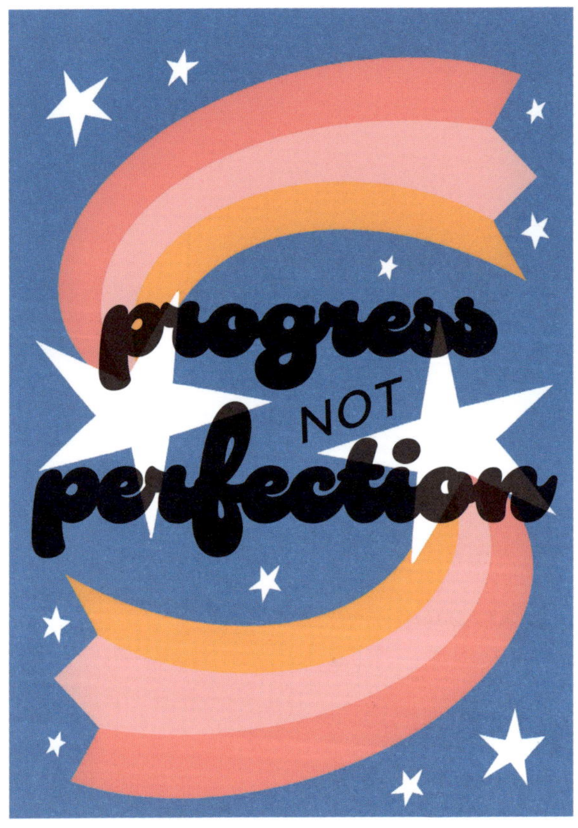

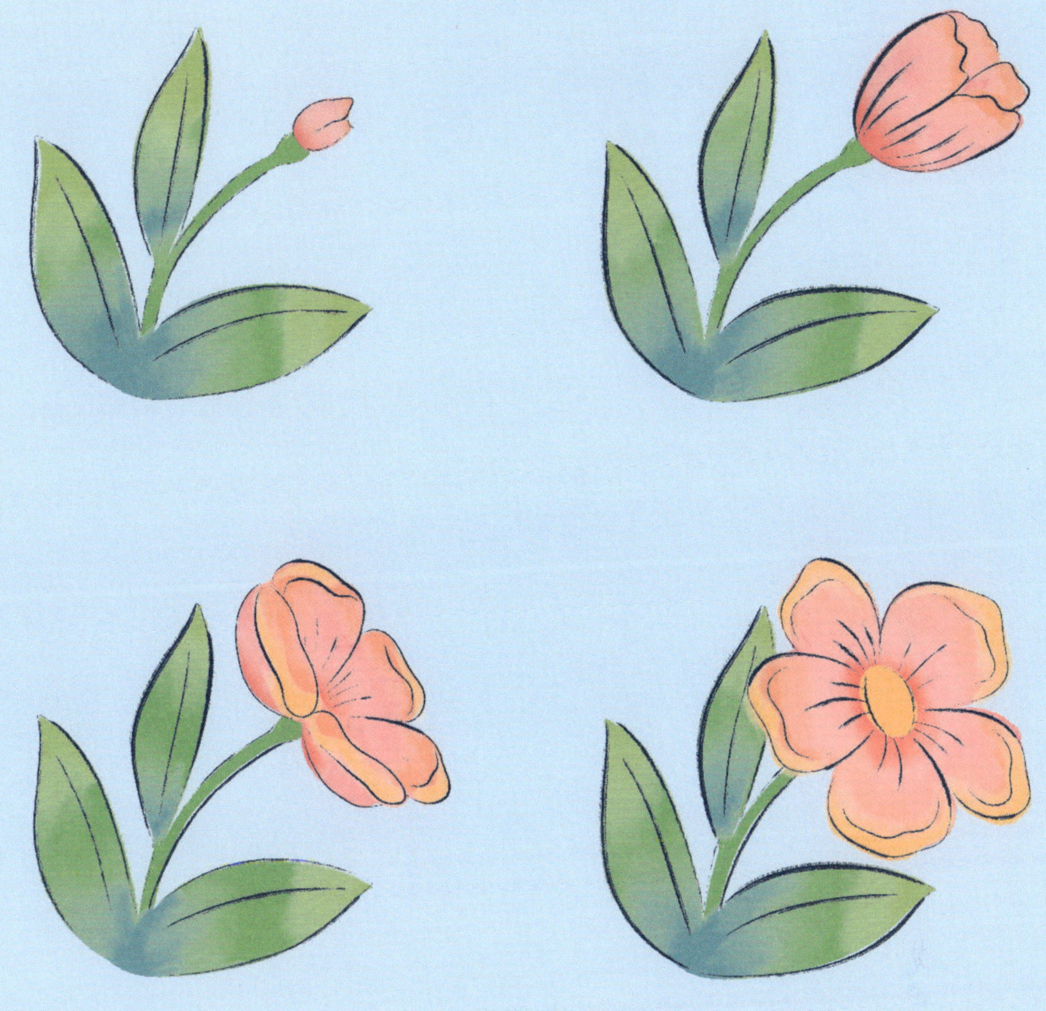

progress not
perfection

HOW TO DRAW KEY ELEMENTS USED IN THIS BOOK

There are a few key illustration motifs that are going to come up a lot in the following projects, so before we begin, I'm going to show you some techniques you can use to help you draw these elements should you choose to include them in your pieces. A great exercise that can help you when trying to figure out your own personal drawing style is to practise drawing an object using different levels of detail and simplicity.

DRAWING REALISTICALLY OR ABSTRACTLY

Drawing in a more detailed, realistic style is a great practice if you want to work on your general drawing skills, and to get a better understanding of shape, light, shade and colour. However, drawing in a simpler, abstract or more cartoon-like style may allow you to let your creativity flow with more ease, and allow you to draw with a bit more freedom and personality.

Practising realism as a starting point in drawing can help you draw an object more abstractly, as the aim in abstract art is to try to convey more of the essence of an object or place than its literal appearance. A great way to work out the essence of something, is to first analyze and understand it in its realistic form. Practising drawing from a more realistic perspective first may help you to more easily abstract it into a simpler form, while still conveying the core of that object.

In the following sections, I will show you how to create simple motifs, beginning with the basics and then adding more detail, which should give you a range of approaches to choose from.

HOW TO DRAW FLOWERS

Flowers are a great metaphor for so many things in life, and are a great, simple way to add interest and colour into your artwork. Here is how you can draw a simple flower, and how you can add more detail to it depending on the style that would best suit your project.

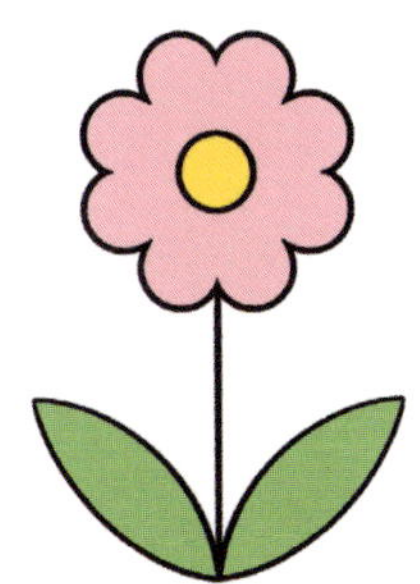

Beginning with the most basic interpretation of a flower, we are going to sketch the basic parts of the flower: the stem, leaves, petals and centre. In this example, the flower is standing perfectly upright; there is symmetry to the left and right side, and there is no variation between the leaves or petals.

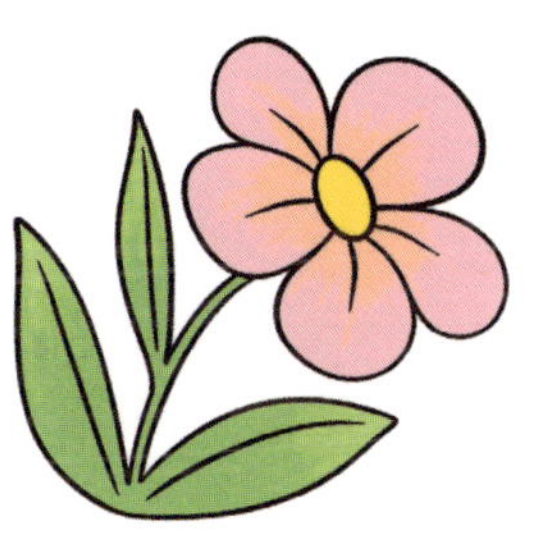

For a more detailed flower, we can make each petal and leaf a slightly different size and shape, which will give the flower a more natural, asymmetrical appearance. To add further detail, we will also add some small flicks to the centre of each petal and leaf to give them more depth and movement.

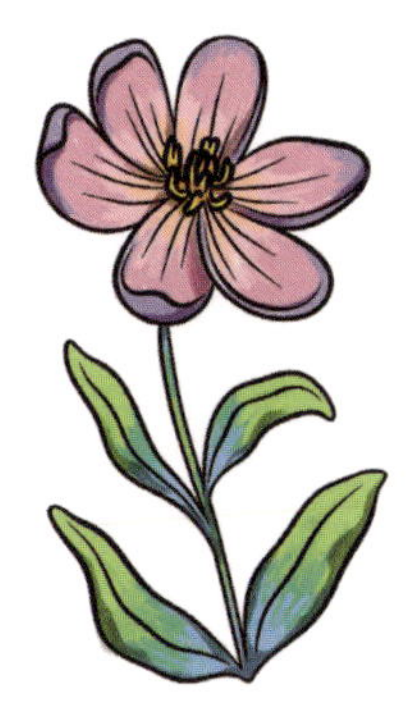

Finally, for a more realistic flower, we will further vary the shape and size of each petal and leaf, focusing on adding more detail to the central part of the petal, as well as some more linework to give the petal more natural movement. You may find it helpful to refer to a reference image when drawing a more realistic flower, as it will help you learn where to add shadows, depth and detail.

HOW TO DRAW LEAVES

Leaves are a wonderful way to add a sense of movement into your pieces. As with the flowers, we will begin a simpler interpretation before adding more details and depth.

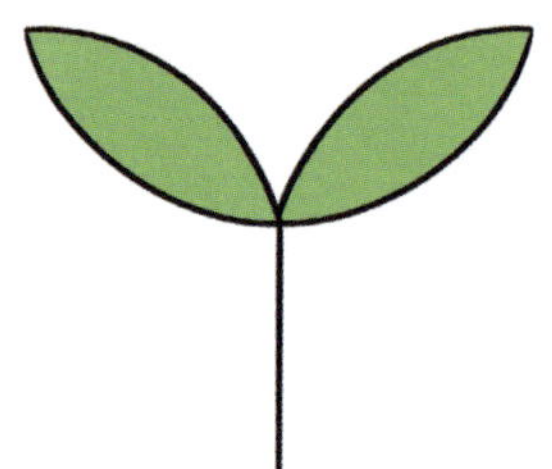

For a simple leaf, draw a sprig with just two leaves. Like the flower, the leaves here have perfect symmetry.

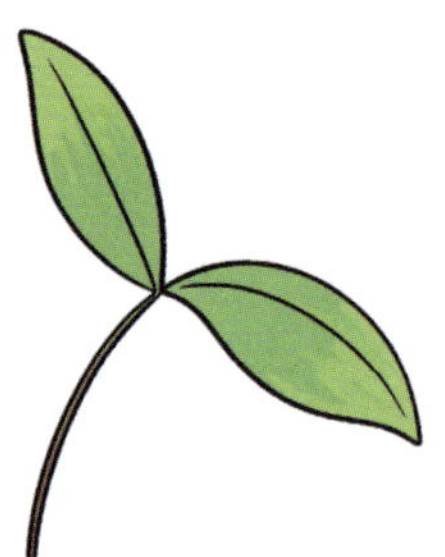

For a leaf with a bit more of a natural shape, add some more curves and soft edges to give the leaves and stems a more realistic feel. Note that the two leaves are still the same size and rough shape, and are drawn using smooth lines, but are less symmetrical.

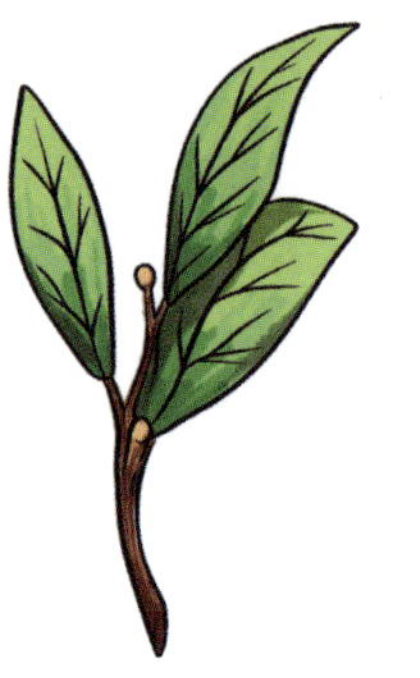

Finally, for a more realistic leaf, focus on adding a mixture of thinner and fatter line strokes to add more intricate details to the leaves (such as the veins at the centre of the leaves). You can also add more curvature lines to give the impression of light and depth on the stem and leaves.

HOW TO DRAW SUNS

Adding facial features to objects is something that I like to experiment with in my drawing, so, in this example, we are going to look at adding facial features to our suns to give them a bit of character.

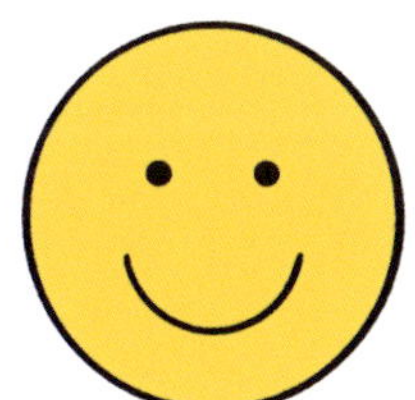

To draw a basic sun, draw a circle shape, and add a very simple smiley face as the facial features.

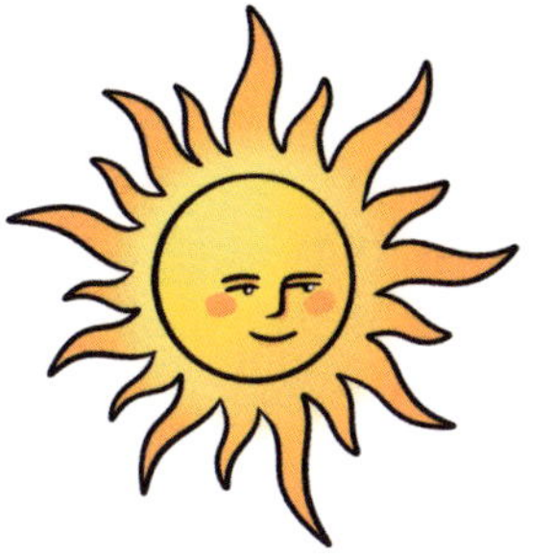

For more detail, add some rays of light around the circle, and add more detail to the face. You could use a photo of yourself or loved one as a reference photo to give you some guidance as to where to place your lines.

To depict a more realistic or detailed sun, we can try blurring the edges of the sunshine to give it a glowing appearance in a more natural way.

HOW TO DRAW MOUNTAINS

For this exercise, we are going to be drawing a small mountain range, which is a motif that can be added to your pieces to create depth, perspective and a sense of adventure.

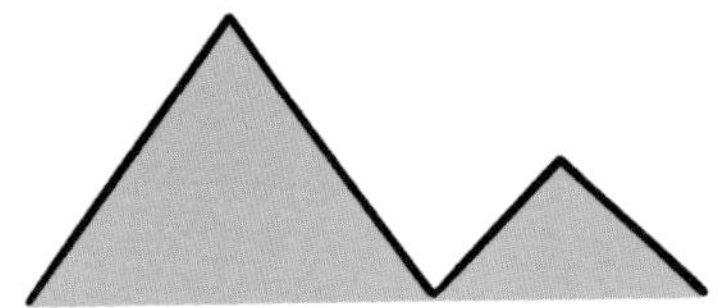

To begin, draw two, basic triangle shapes as your outline. Each triangle needs to be a different size so that it's still clear to the viewer that it is a mountain range.

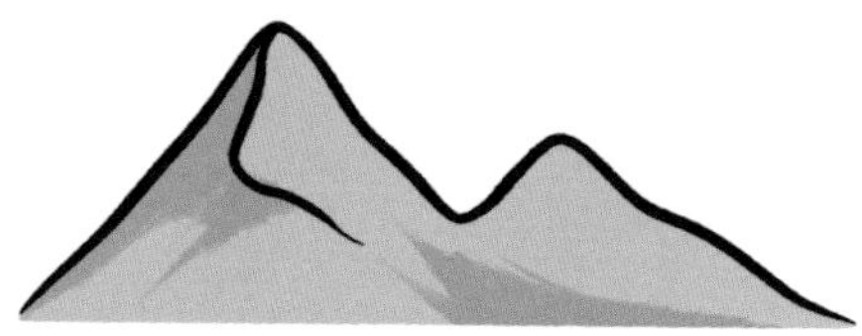

To add more detail, soften the lines of your triangles and add some more jagged lines to the surface of the mountains. This shows more of the rocky texture and gives the landscape more dimension.

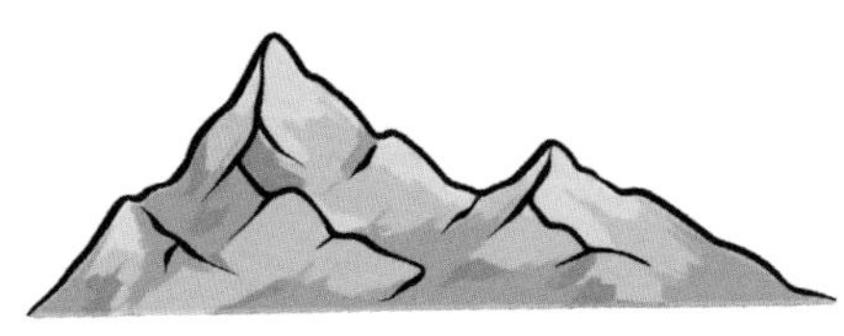

Finally, you can create even more texture by adding further variation to the mountain edges, and more fine line detail to the sloping areas. This will help you increase the three-dimensional element of the drawing. For help identifying where to place your lines, look to a reference photo to help guide you.

HOW TO DRAW CLOUDS

Clouds can bring a feeling of softness and calm or drama and depth to a piece, depending on the weather.

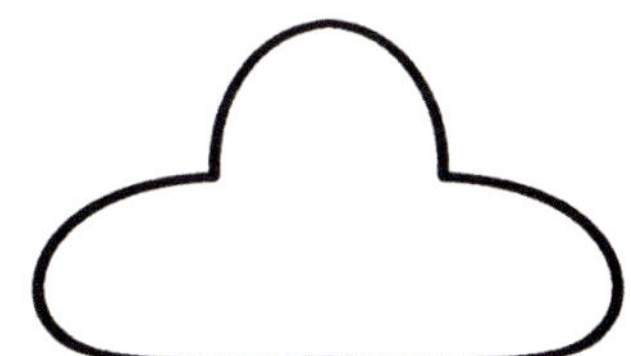

To begin drawing a basic cloud, draw a rounded, three-sided shape that is symmetrical on both sides, and flat at the bottom.

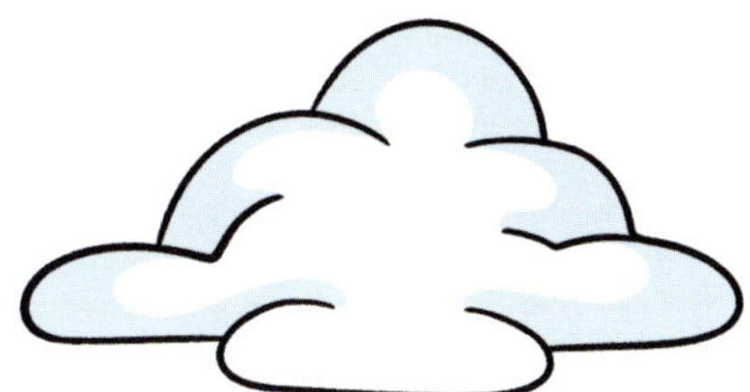

For a more detailed cloud, create more variation between the two sides of the cloud and add more depth by including some detail lines around the edges.

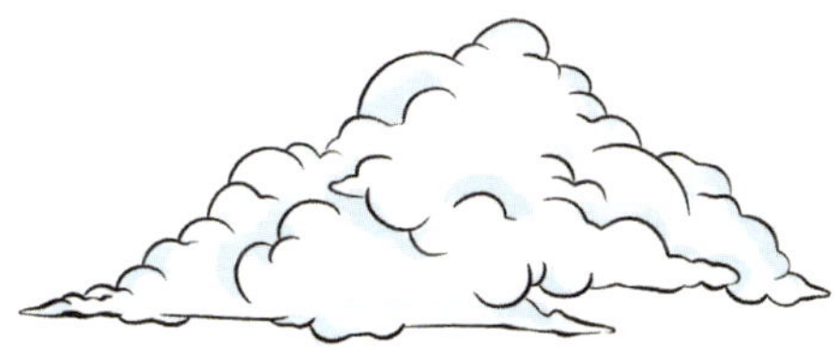

Finally, for an even more realistic looking cloud, experiment by adding more jagged linework to complement the softer curves, and ensure there is no symmetry. If you're struggling, look outside and sketch a cloud you see, or take a reference photo to work from next time you spot one you like.

PAIRING DIFFERENT ELEMENTS TOGETHER

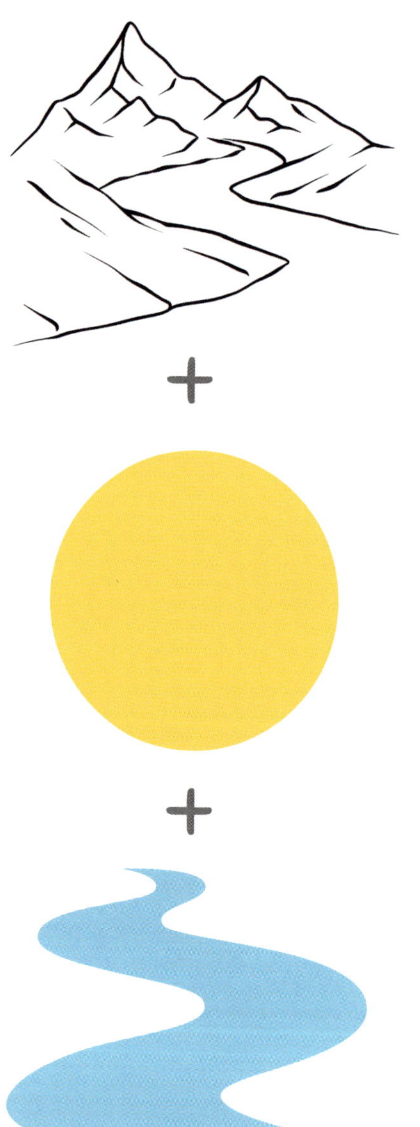

Now we are going to look at how you can pair different elements together in one drawing. You may think that if you have created a realistic flower you need to also draw any other elements in the same style. However, this doesn't have to be the case, and you can create really interesting effects by pairing different styles together. Here is an example of a piece I created to show you how this can work.

In this example, I chose to draw a piece using a mountain range and a sun. I wanted the mountains to be the foreground element, so I used some detail to make it eye-catching to the viewer. I also wanted to use the sun as an opportunity to add some abstract elements into the artwork, so I used a basic yellow circle, making it much larger than the mountains. To add some more colour, I decided to add a river into the landscape, so I chose to colour block this area in blue to help balance the abstracted elements.

Experimenting with contrasts is a simple way to add interest to your work. By using different levels of realism between foreground and background, and playing with scale in this way, the resulting piece is more dynamic and visually engaging.

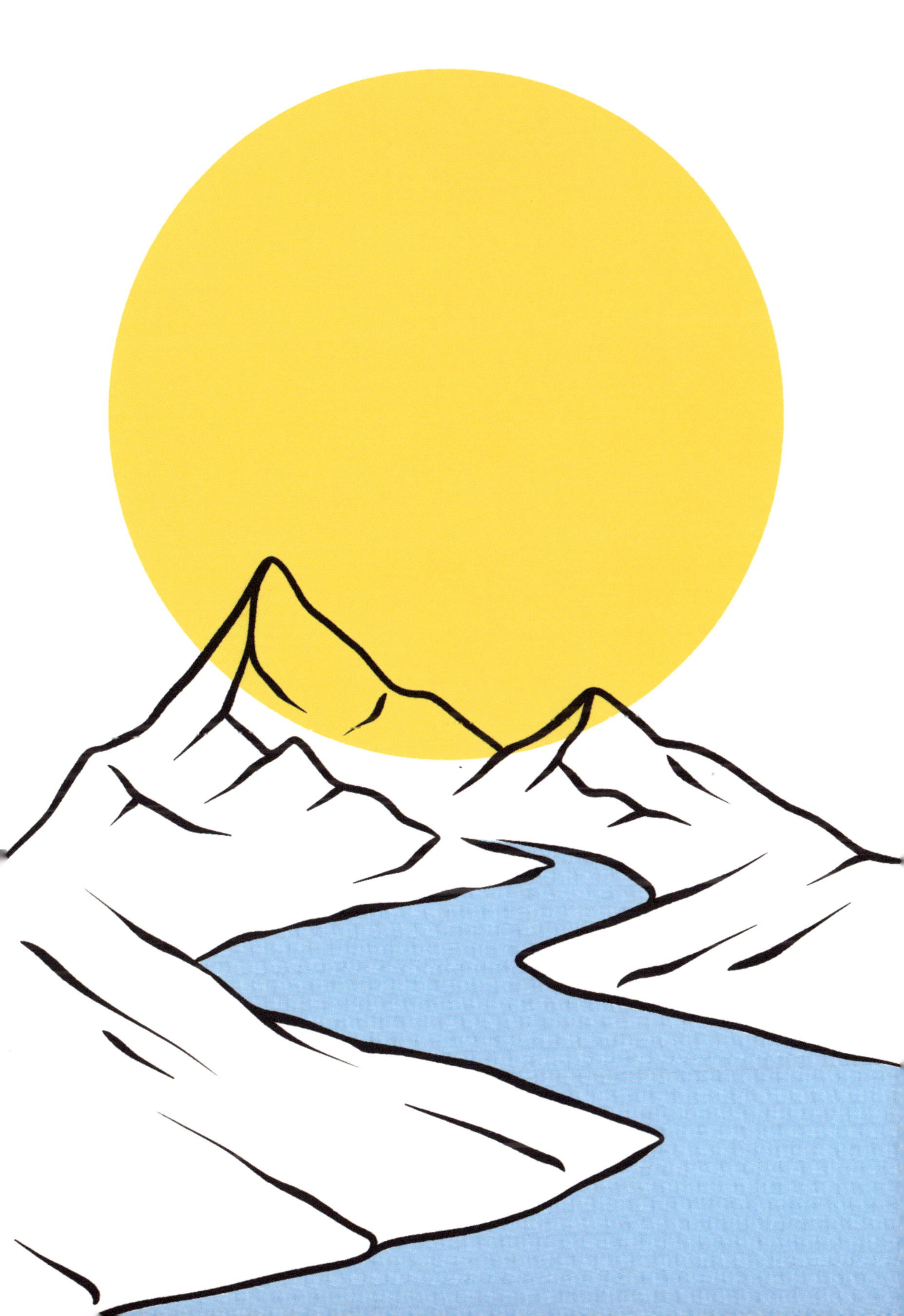

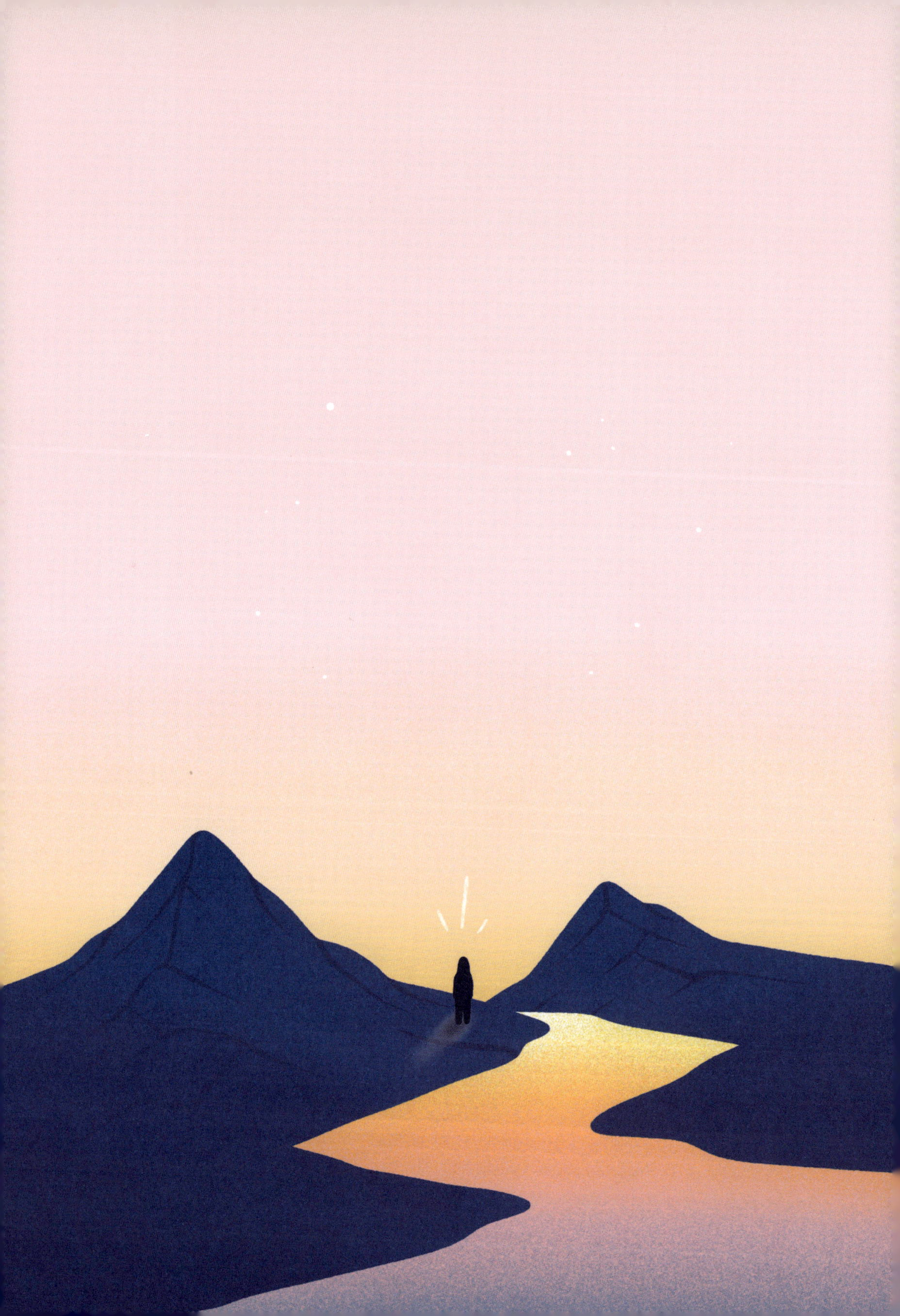

MANTRA PROJECTS

Now that we have gone through all of the techniques you need to know, and asked yourself all the questions you need to ask before putting pen to paper, we can introduce our projects. These have been sorted into the themes of **calm, uplift** and **inspire**.
You do not need to work through them in order, and the projects have been placed together in this way so that you can decide which project you would like to work on based on what you're feeling or want to feel at the time.

Before you begin a new project, here is a helpful list of questions and prompts to run through. Filling out this checklist will help you work more efficiently while holding on to that sense of fun and play.

- ☆ What colours do you think would suit each piece?
- ☆ Do you want to use more colour in one drawing than the other?
- ☆ What media do you think would suit each piece?
- ☆ Could you use the same media to produce two different effects?
- ☆ What lettering do you think would suit each piece?
- ☆ Do you think you should use different-sized lettering on each piece?
- ☆ Do you think you could use the same composition for both pieces?
- ☆ Could you use the same illustrative aspects but rearrange them to suit each piece?

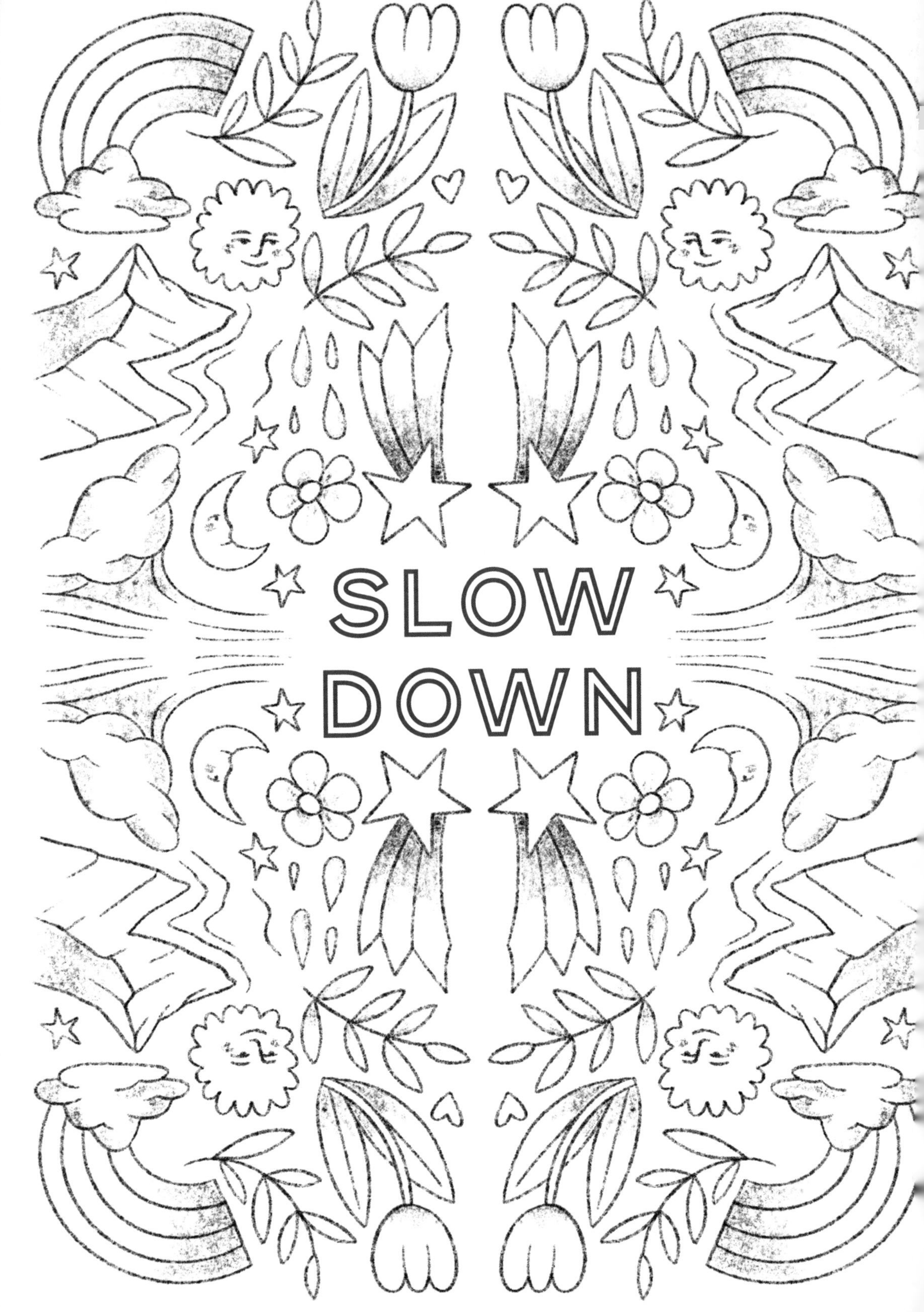
SLOW
DOWN

SLOW DOWN

In today's fast-paced world, it is important to give some time to slow things down and check in with yourself. Learning how to slow down can have a positive impact on your ability to focus and think mindfully, and can even help with your creativity.

For this calming mantra, we are going to be using nature motifs to illustrate the idea of 'slowing down'. Many people find spending time in nature a calming experience, as it gives them a break from the busyness of day-to-day life, and allows them to notice things that they might otherwise miss. We will be using symmetry in this piece, as this will give the artwork a sense of balance, and will also act as a metaphor for creating balance in our own lives.

Take this opportunity while working on this mantra project to think about the small things in nature that bring you joy, and let them inspire you to slow down sometimes.

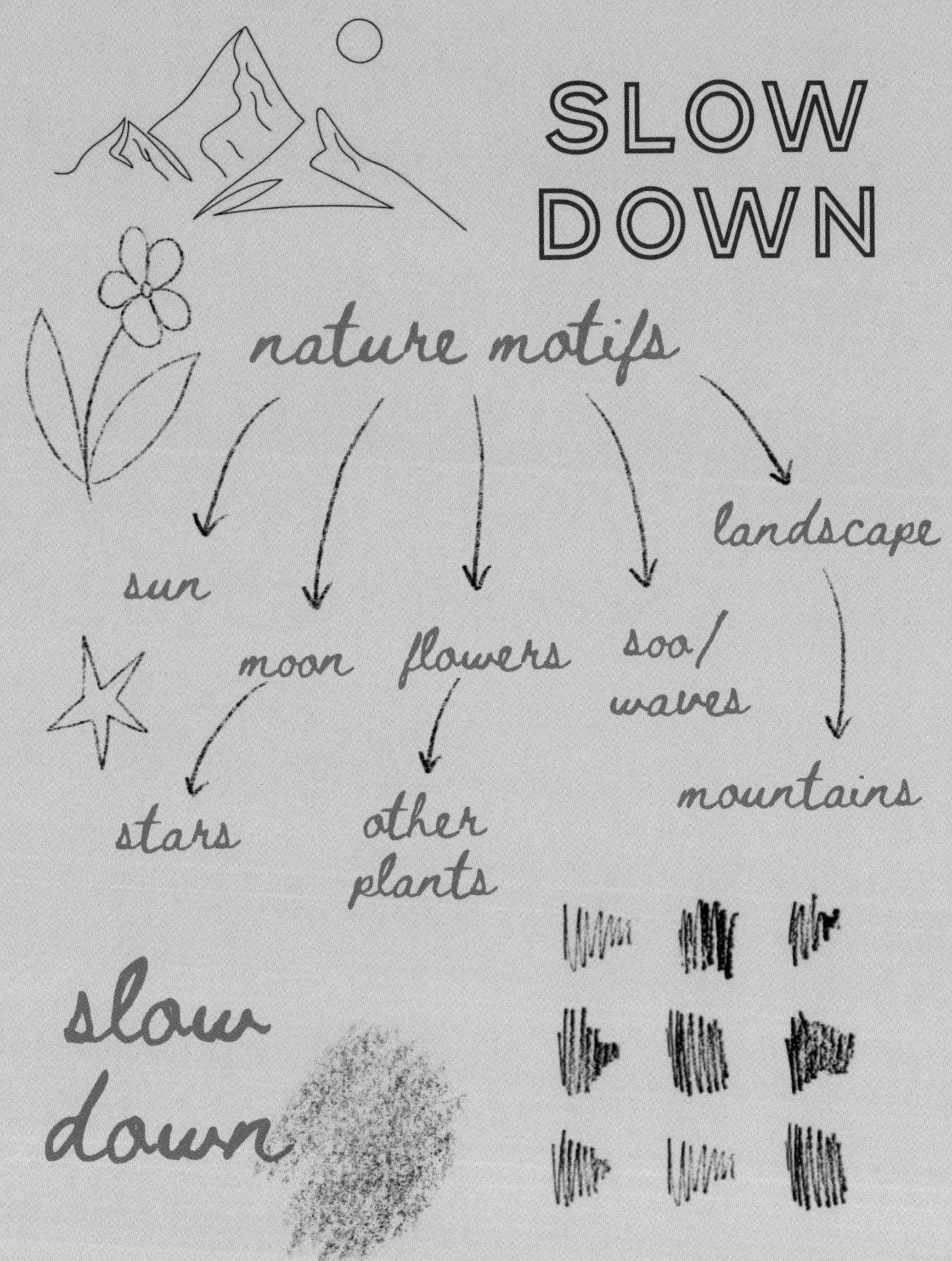

SLOW DOWN
nature motifs
sun
moon
flowers
soo/
waves
landscape
stars
other
plants
mountains
slow
down

MANTRA MOOD BOARD

I'm going to be using black pencil for this piece, as the good thing about using pencil is that you can use different amounts of pressure to get different intensities of the colour you are using.

I want the nature aspects I'm using to stand out equally, so I'm going to draw them all at roughly the same scale. I also want to experiment with symmetry in this mantra illustration, so I have chosen to include just a handful of small motifs in this piece, which will help prevent the layout from feeling disorganized and jumbled together.

As this mantra will feature small motifs, the lettering will need to stand out while also being in keeping with the style of the illustration, so I'm going to use block capital letters.

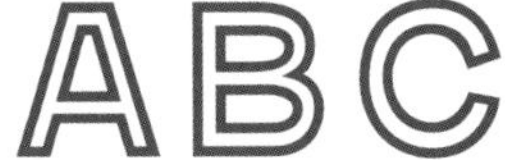

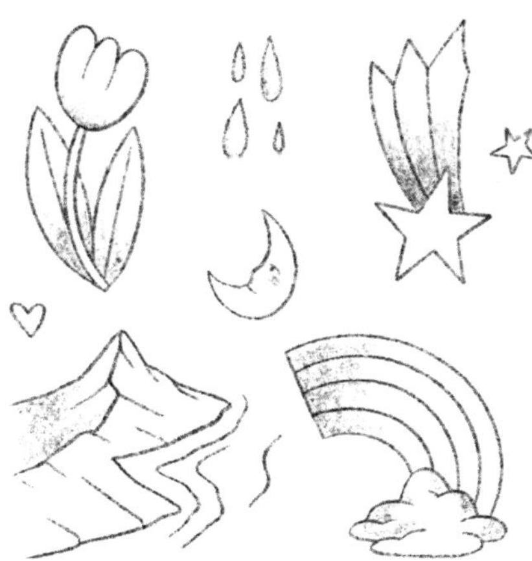

USING SYMMETRY

There are many different types of symmetry that you can experiment with both digitally and practically when drawing. Here, we are going to look into a few of these options that will be used throughout this book. On the next page, I will teach you how to create symmetry using Photoshop and practical methods.

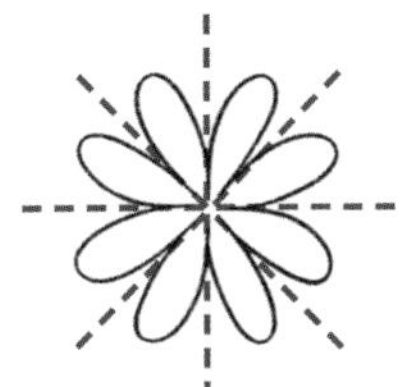

RADIAL SYMMETRY

This creates an arrangement around a central point, where the pattern is consistent and repeated in each segment. When creating radial symmetry in Photoshop you will have the option to choose how many segments to include. I usually use six segments, but if you spend some time experimenting with this feature you may find you prefer to use a different setting.

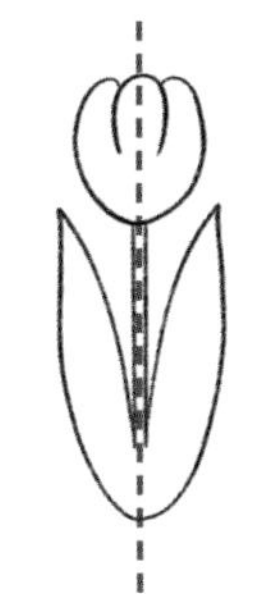

VERTICAL SYMMETRY

This creates a dividing line down the centre of your canvas that will mirror your image vertically.

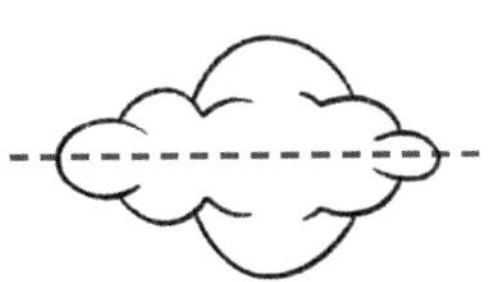

HORIZONTAL SYMMETRY

Horizontal symmetry creates a dividing line across the middle of your canvas that will mirror your image horizontally.

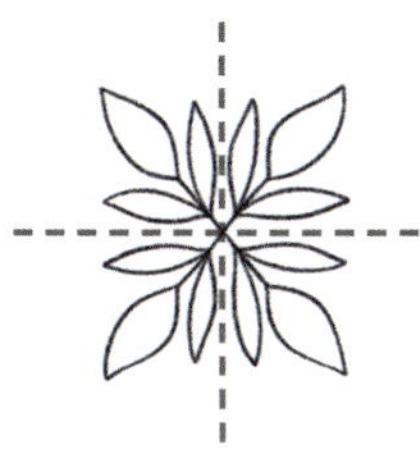

DUAL AXIS SYMMETRY

This will create both vertical and horizontal dividing lines on your canvas. It will split your canvas into four so that your image will mirror itself both vertically and horizontally.

How to Create Symmetry Digitally

When you click on the 'Brush' tool to begin your drawing, you will see an icon that looks like a butterfly at the end of the options in the top toolbar. If you click on this icon, you will see a drop-down menu with options for all of the different types of symmetry you can experiment with. We are using dual axis symmetry in this particular project, but I encourage you to play around with the other options available here and see what effects you can create!

How to Create Symmetry Practically

To use symmetry when drawing by hand, draw your line or lines of symmetry lightly on a piece of paper (see the previous page for guidance), and then draw your design in one of these sections. Once you are happy with your design, cover your paper with a piece of tracing paper and trace over your design using a soft-leaded pencil (a B lead pencil would work well). Once you have completed your tracing, flip your tracing paper over so it is in the centre of the next section of your paper, and draw over your tracing using an HB pencil so it transfers onto the paper. If you are using quadrant or radial symmetry, keep adding your traced design to your spaces until your page is filled. Once this is done, you can remove the tracing paper and go over your drawing to clean up the lines.

COMPOSITION

This piece is a calming mantra, so I wanted it to feel softer and convey the mantra message in a more subtle way. I chose to use a pencil brush for this whole piece as it creates more of an imperfect 'doodling' feel that aligns with the mantra message of 'slowing down'. To create my mantra, I used Photoshop, following the steps on pages 16–23 to prepare for my project. The practical media alternative for this artwork would be pencil and tracing paper.

ELEMENTS

I set my canvas symmetry to 'Quadrant' for this artwork, and drew the outlines for my motifs in the top left corner of my canvas, which was then copied symmetrically into the other three spaces. Once I was happy with my outlines I added another layer below the outline layer, again set this layer to 'Quadrant' symmetry, and lightly added some shading to each of the motifs to add a bit more detail.

If you are drawing this mantra by hand, you'll need to split your canvas into four (using a ruler to be accurate), draw your motif outlines in one corner, and then follow the tracing method on page 53. Once your tracing is complete, you can go over the traced sections to clean up the lines, then add your shading to complete.

TEXT

I used an outlined lettering for this piece, as the illustrations are quite simple and drawn lightly. I chose the font 'Fenwick', as I felt it wouldn't stand out too much in the piece. I placed it in the middle of the piece as a focal point, and sized it to fit in the space created by the illustration using the steps on page 22.

If you are writing your mantra by hand, I recommend lightly sketching the lettering in capitals, then creating your outlined letters from there as it will be easier to keep your letter size consistent this way.

1.

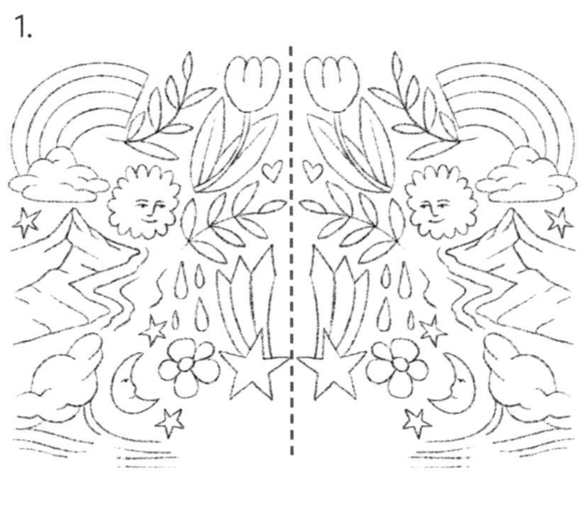

2.

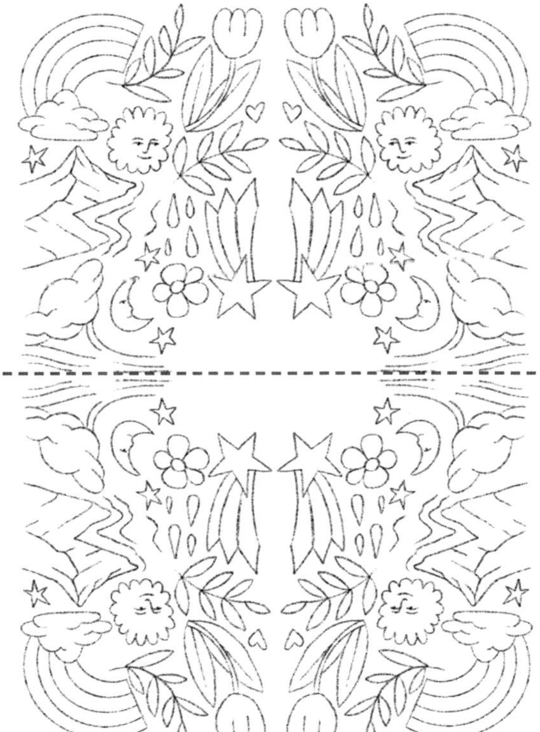

3.

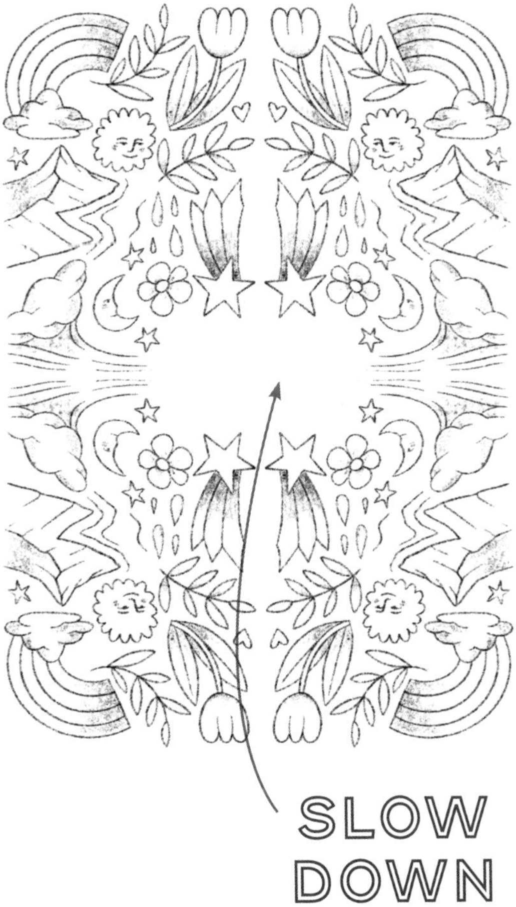

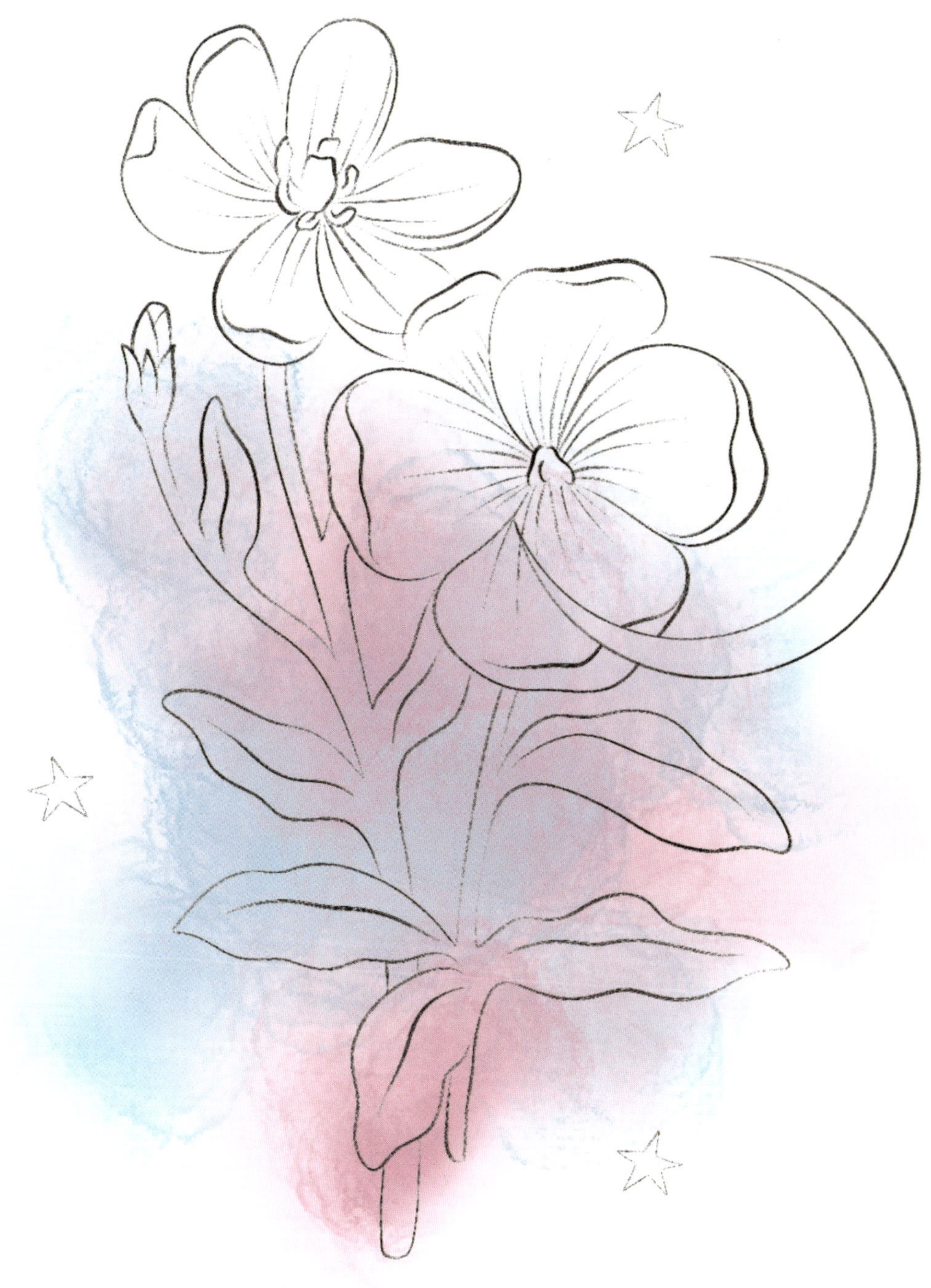

take care of yourself

TAKE CARE
OF YOURSELF

Taking care of yourself, or self-care, means making time to do the things to maintain and improve your physical and mental wellbeing. Finding the time to do this around a busy schedule can be difficult, but even the smallest acts of self-care in your daily routine can make a big difference, and have positive impacts on your overall wellbeing.

Simply checking in with yourself and asking yourself how you are feeling emotionally, mentally and physically is a great first step. Self-care won't look the same for everyone, as we all have different likes and pastimes that bring us joy. So whether it's making time for your hobbies, going for a walk in nature or simply making sure you're getting enough sleep, prioritize doing anything you can to feel cared for, no matter how small.

This calming exercise has been designed to allow you to experiment with looser and more gentle techniques, adding to the canvas freely and not being too careful about things looking a certain way. So, make some space for yourself where you can relax, and let your creativity flow.

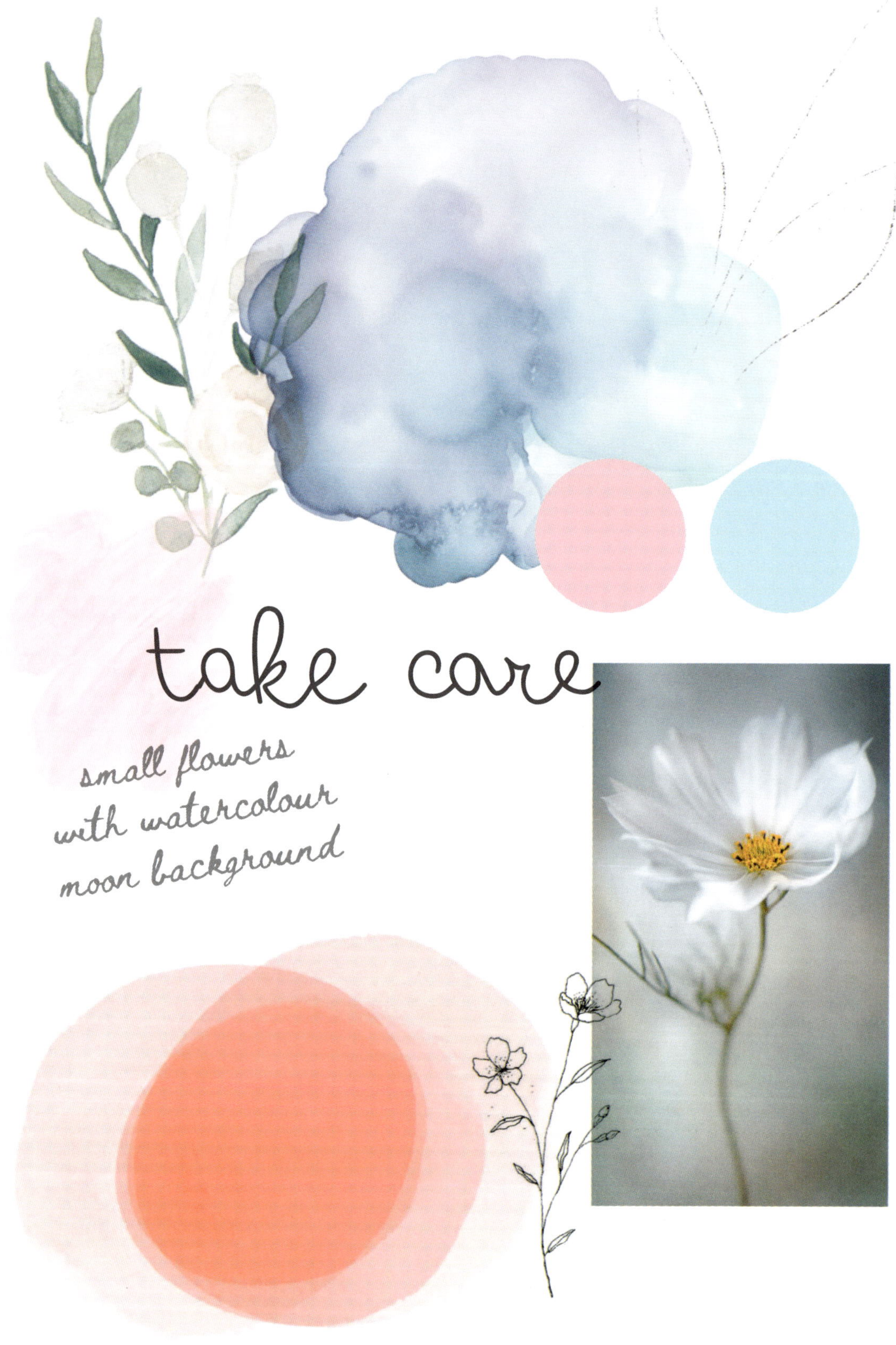

take care
small flowers
with watercolour
moon background

MANTRA MOOD BOARD

For this mantra artwork, we're going to use delicate flowers to represent taking care of something. Using fine lines on top of a watercolour effect, we will focus on keeping this piece simple and soothing to best evoke the idea of taking care of yourself.

For this piece, I'm going to be using light pink and light blue. I find these colours to have a calming and peaceful effect on me, but if there are colours you feel would be more suitable for your interpretation, feel free to use them!

To highlight the delicate nature of the flowers, I am going to be drawing my illustrations using light pencil strokes.

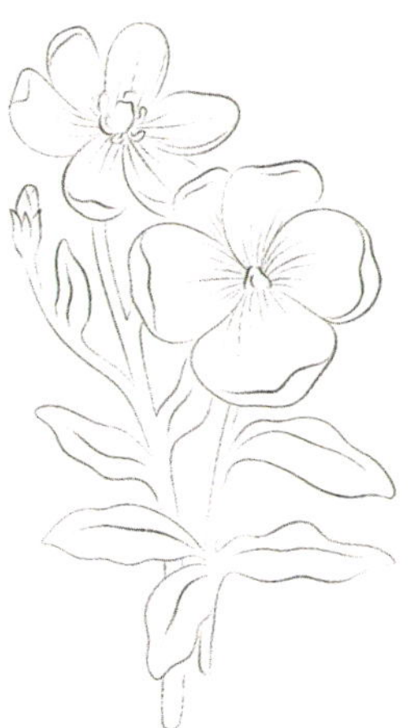

Alongside the flowers, I'm also going to be including a moon and stars to symbolize guidance and inspiration.

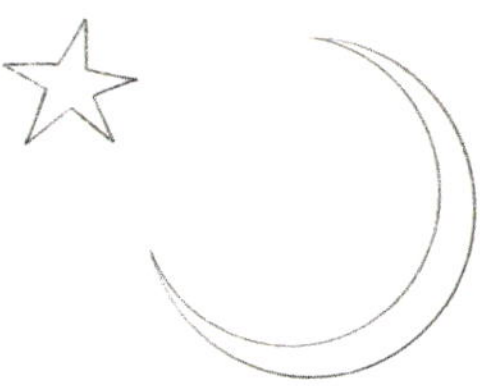

As this mantra is a bit longer, I'm going to be using key words with a big, bold font to help break the wording up, and add some more interest to the artwork. I will also be using handwritten text in the same style as the stars to tie the piece together.

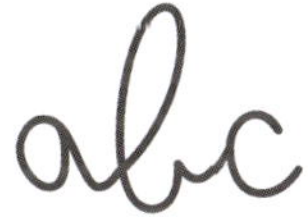

USING WATERCOLOUR WASH BACKGROUNDS

A watercolour wash is a great way to add subtle, muted colours to the background of your mantra illustrations. As the colour goes on to the page with a more transparent appearance, you can take your time building up the layers of colour until you are happy with how it looks.

SPLASH WASH

A splash wash is a type of watercolour wash that gives the appearance of splashes of paint. It offers a looser and more random application of colour on the page, and is a great choice for when you want to create a background with a bit more interest.

How to Create

Select the 'Brush' picker (see page 21). Then, scroll down to the bottom and click on the 'Legacy Brushes' drop-down box to open this list of options. If this does not appear, you will need to click the settings icon (which looks like a cog) in the 'Brush' picker box, and click 'Legacy Brushes'. This will install the brushes, which should now appear on the scroll down list. Once you have found 'Legacy Brushes', scroll down to 'Wet Media Brushes', then scroll down through this list until you find the watercolour brushes.

Using the 'Light Watercolour Brush', click and move your mouse in circular motions on your canvas to get your first colour on the page. This brush creates quite a natural effect of layering the colour if you go over it again, so you can build up your layers of colour until you are happy with how it looks. Once you have finished with your first colour, create a new layer set to 'Multiply' (see page 18), and repeat the same process with your second colour.

To create a splash wash using watercolour paints, get some water on your brush and brush the areas where you want your background to be. Then, add more water to your brush, dip your brush into one of your chosen colours, and brush it onto the page.

Before the first colour dries fully, repeat the same process with your second colour using a clean brush. You don't want the first colour to be completely dried, as you want the two colours to blend together in some areas. I recommend using a lot of water with this technique as it will allow you to slowly build up the layers until you are happy with how your background looks.

GRADIENT WASH

A gradient wash gives the appearance of slowly transitioning from one colour to another. If you would like to achieve a background with a more uniform composition, try a gradient wash where the colours blend from one to the other across or down the page.

How to Create

As with the splash wash, we are going to use the watercolour brush presets, this time using the 'Watercolour Heavy Loaded' brush. Using one colour on your brush, fill one half of your canvas with that colour, then fill the other half of your canvas with the second colour. Next, right click on the 'Brush' tool icon and click on the 'Mixer Brush' tool. Then, select the 'Light Watercolour Brush' tool and blend the two colours together.

To create a gradient wash using watercolour paints, load your brush up with water, and brush across the whole page. Once your page is covered with a light layer of water, add your first colour to your brush, and fill the top half of your page with this colour. Start at the very top of the page, where you want the colour to be strongest, and blend down towards the middle. Now, with a clean brush, use your second colour to fill the bottom half of your page. You want this colour to be strongest at the bottom of the page, so start from the bottom and work upwards, towards the middle. Finally, to ensure the two colours blend in the middle of the page, take a clean brush, dip it in water, and brush between the two colours until you are happy with the blend.

COMPOSITION

To create this mantra, I used Photoshop, following the steps on pages 16–23 to prepare for my project. The practical media alternative for this artwork would be watercolour paint for the background, and either pencil or a very fine point liner for the flower outlines and mantra lettering.

BACKGROUND

To create my splash wash background, I used the process described on page 60. Using a watercolour brush, I started by applying pink paint to my canvas on one layer (with the layer set to 'Multiply'), and then added blue paint to a separate layer (also to 'Multiply').

If you are creating this artwork practically, follow the steps for using watercolour paints for splash wash on page 61.

TEXT

I wanted to use a light, delicate font for this artwork to complement the style of the rest of the piece, so I chose to use the 'Bimbo Pro Finetip' font to work well with the other elements.

If you are creating this piece practically, I would recommend using the same pencil or pen that you are going to draw your flowers with to write your mantra message, as this will help to make the piece look cohesive. When writing, you can try to use a calligraphic style, which will have a similar appearance to the writing in the example artwork. Or, you could just use lowercase writing, which would also work for this piece.

ELEMENTS

I used a pencil brush to draw a pansy and a buttercup, as these are quite small and delicate flowers. When drawing, try to not use much pressure when drawing with a pencil (digitally or practically), as you want the style of this artwork to be light and to reflect the delicate nature of the flowers.

I also included the moon and some stars in this piece. As the moon is in the foreground, I added this to the page first. Remember to use the same amount of pressure to the page when drawing all of the elements so that one doesn't stand out more than the others.

1.

2.

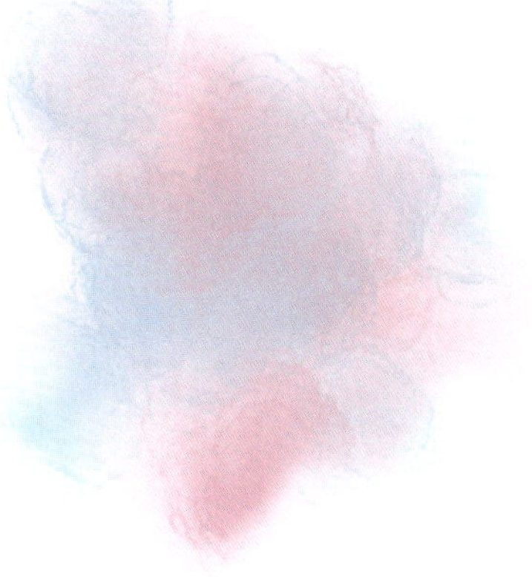

3.

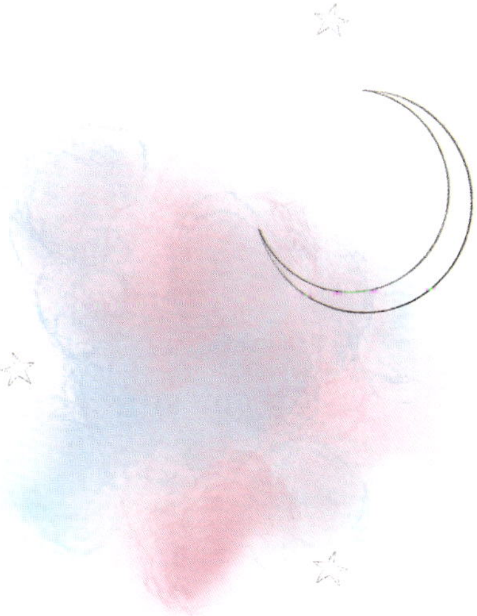

4.

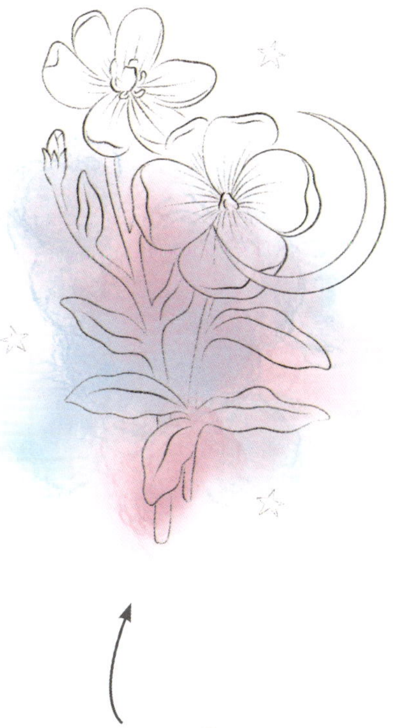

take care of yourself

be the
ENERGY
you want to
ATTRACT

BE THE ENERGY YOU WANT TO ATTRACT

We all possess our own unique energies, and the power to use positive energy to invite the positive things that we want to bring into our lives. We attract what we put out into the world, and this mantra is a great reminder to take some time to think about the things you wish to receive in life, and how you can practise radiating the energy you wish to receive in return.

For this manifesting mantra, we'll be exploring the idea of using auras to visualize your energies, and using the tools of blurring and gradient colours to do this. As well as working through the mantra artwork given in the example, you will have the opportunity to create your own personal version of this artwork, with your own aura composition.

While working through this project, I invite you to take this opportunity to check in with yourself – reflect on the energies you are putting out into the world right now, and think about whether this is the energy you want to be welcoming into your life. If the answer is no, I gently encourage you to use the time spent working through this project to think about what changes you could make to realign yourself and take steps towards removing those negative things that may be affecting you. Remember to be kind to yourself, and that taking small steps towards change is totally okay.

MANTRA MOOD BOARD

For this project, we're going to be conveying the idea of 'energy' by creating an abstracted interpretation of an aura, or ball of energy. Using blurred gradients, and other simple illustrative elements, you'll be focusing on the spiritual significance of your chosen colour palette, and how you can use colour to attract specific energies into your life through your art.

For my interpretation of this mantra, I'm going to be using three colours: pink to represent love, orange to inspire creativity, and yellow to increase confidence. You can use as many or as few colours as you like, and you can find out more about how to select the right colours for your project on page 24.

I want the main feature of this illustration to be a soft, gradient background to convey the idea of energy. The blurred colour spreading across the page and blending with the other colours will give it the feeling of motion and energy spreading

and transferring. We'll talk more about how to select and create the perfect gradient on pages 68 and 69.

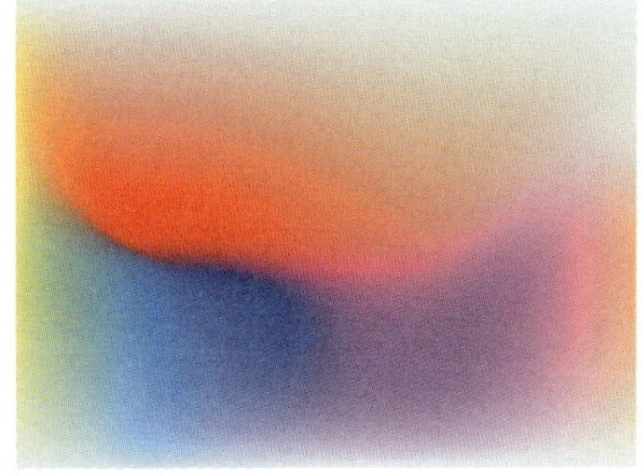

I also want to include some simple stars on my piece to symbolize energy and aspirations.

As this mantra is a bit longer, I'm going to be using key words with a big, bold font to help break the wording up, and add some more interest to the artwork. I will also be using handwritten text in the same style as the stars to tie the piece together.

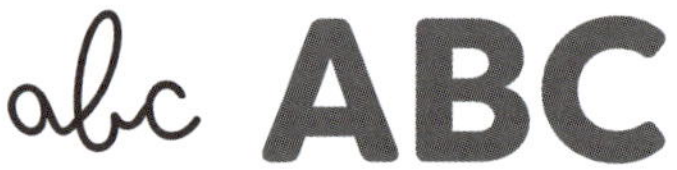

HOW TO FIND YOUR AURA

To begin planning and creating your piece, you're going to select the colour or colours you'd like to work with based on your aura. Your aura is a combination of colours that are affected by your moods and emotions, and could be seen as a visual reaction to the energy you radiate.

As your mood and emotions are changeable, you may want to choose colours to inspire emotions that you would like to feel more (for example, if you want to feel more confident, you could choose yellow), or you may want to pick things that describe your character in a more general sense (for example, if you are generally a caring person, you could choose pink).

To help you figure out your aura, here is a guide to tell you what each colour signifies. You want this mantra illustration to represent you, so include as many colours as you feel resonate with you.

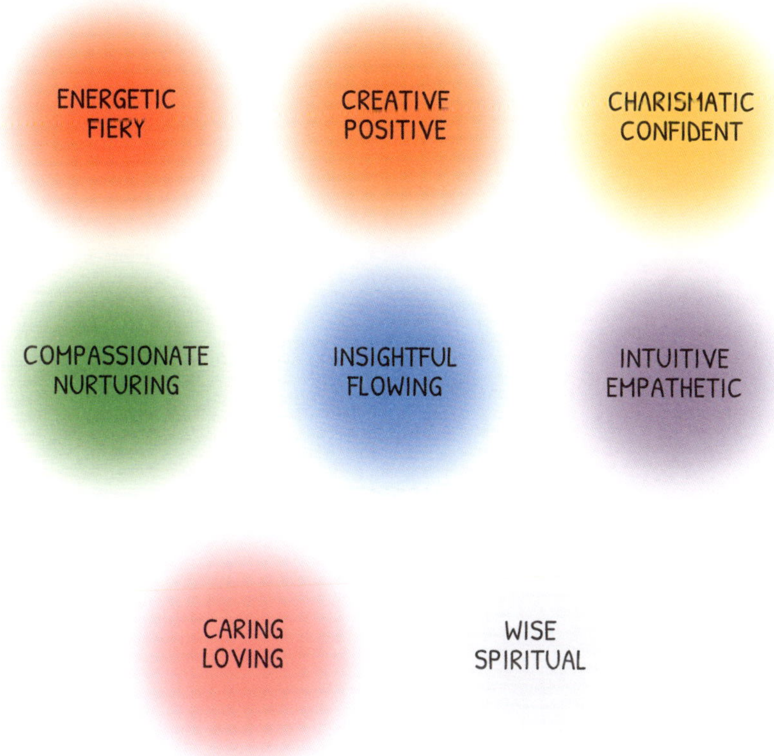

USING GRADIENTS

Once you have selected the colours you'd like to use for your piece, you can plan your gradient background. Gradients are a simple but effective way to utilize colour in your artwork. They create an interesting visual and are a great way to symbolize transition and motion (making it perfect for this manifesting mantra), as the colours transition gradually from one colour to the other.

Below are a few different types of gradients you can use in your project.

LINEAR GRADIENT

In a linear gradient, the colours flow in a single direction from one colour to the other. For example, from left to right, top to bottom or any angle you choose.

How to create

To create a linear gradient in Photoshop, use the 'Brush' tool to apply your two colours evenly on either side of the page on the same layer. Once the colours are down, keep the layer selected and use the 'Gaussian Blur' tool to blur the two colours together and create your gradient. You can play around with the amount of blur you add until you are happy with how it looks.

A simple practical alternative to create a gradient would be to use something like chalk pastels. Add your colours on either side of the page, and use your finger to lightly brush over the surface of the page from one side to the next. This will create a blend between the two colours and produce a blurring effect.

RADIAL GRADIENT

Here, a transition is created between two or more colours that radiate from a single point of origin. The resulting shape will have the appearance of a circle or an ellipse.

How to create

To create a radial gradient in Photoshop, use the 'Paint Bucket' tool to fill your background with one of your colours, and then use the 'Brush' tool or 'Ellipse' tool to create a circle in the centre of the background. Once this is done, follow the same process explained above, using the 'Gaussian Blur' tool to create your desired gradient.

To create a radial gradient using our practical alternative of chalk pastels, start with your inner circle shape, with one colour in the centre of your page, then add the background colour around it. Once complete, use your finger to blend the colours together.

REFLECTED GRADIENT

This gradient resembles a reflection, as it creates a mirrored effect with one colour in the centre of the page, transitioning into another colour on either side of it.

How to create

To create a reflected gradient in Photoshop, use the 'Paint Bucket' tool to fill your background with one of your colours, and then use the 'Brush' tool or 'Rectangle' tool to create a line of your second colour down the centre of the page. Use the 'Gaussian Blur' tool to create your gradient.

To create a reflected gradient with your chalk pastels, start by placing your middle colour on the page, then fill in either side of the page with your second colour. Once done, follow the same process of using your finger to blend.

MULTI-POINT GRADIENT

In a multi-point gradient, the colours aren't placed uniformly on the page. For example, when using a two-colour gradient, the appearance of the gradient will look like one colour as the background, with the other colour spreading out from multiple points on the page.

How to create

To create a multi-point gradient in Photoshop, use the 'Paint Bucket' tool to fill in your background with one of your colours, then use the 'Brush' tool to randomly add spots of your second colour to the background. Once this is done, follow the same blurring process to create your gradient using the 'Gaussian Blur' tool.

To create this style of gradient practically using chalk pastels, start by placing your random spots of colour on the page, then fill in the rest of the page using your second colour. Once this is completed, use your finger to blend the colours.

COMPOSITION

Once you have decided on your aura colours, and any additional illustrative elements that you may wish to include in your mantra artwork, you can begin to assemble your piece.

For this mantra, I used Photoshop, following the steps on pages 16–23 to prepare for my project. The practical media alternative for this artwork would be to use paper and an airbrush if you wanted to recreate the same fine spray of colour, however, you could achieve the same effect with more accessible methods such as fine spray paint (make sure you do this outside), watercolour paint or chalk pastels on canvas or paper.

BACKGROUND

To start my piece, I began with a white background. You'll need to work in layers to create the visual of the colours blending together and overlapping, so make sure you have all of your layer types set to 'Multiply' for however many colours you are using.

Selecting the background layer, create a circular shape with the 'Ellipse' tool.

Once this is on the page, use the 'Gaussian Blur' tool to create the desired amount of blurring you would like your background to have. Repeat this process with the rest of your colours until you are happy with how your background looks.

If you are creating your artwork using a practical medium like watercolour, you'll also need to work in layers. Using just water on your brush, create a rough circle shape for the first colour. Once this is complete, add a small amount of watercolour paint on your brush, and place it on the page somewhere around the centre of your water circle. The pigment will then spread through the water, which will create that blurred-edge effect we see in this example artwork. Once this first colour layer is partially dry, you can then repeat the same process with your second colour. You don't want to wait until the first layer has dried completely, because you want the different colours to slightly blend together at the edges. The amount of water on the page will determine how blurred the edges of the paint appear, so you may want to use a separate piece of paper to experiment with the ratio of water to paint to achieve your desired look.

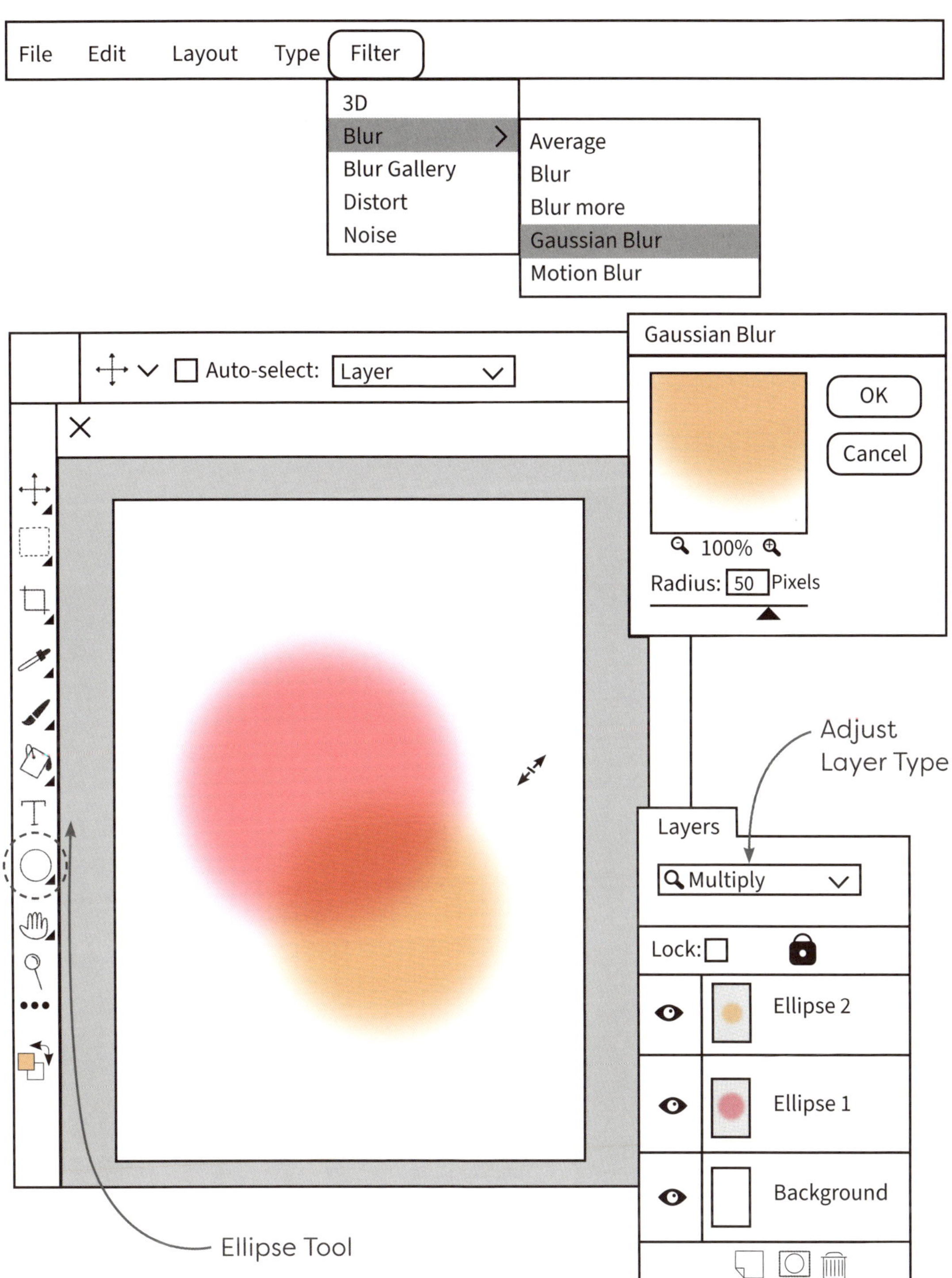

File
Edit
Layout
Type
Filter
3D
Blur
Blur Gallery
Distort
Noise
Average
Blur
Blur more
Gaussian Blur
Motion Blur
Auto-select:
Layer
Gaussian Blur
OK
Cancel
100%
Radius: 50 Pixels
Adjust Layer Type
Layers
Multiply
Lock:
Ellipse 2
Ellipse 1
Background
Ellipse Tool

1.

2.

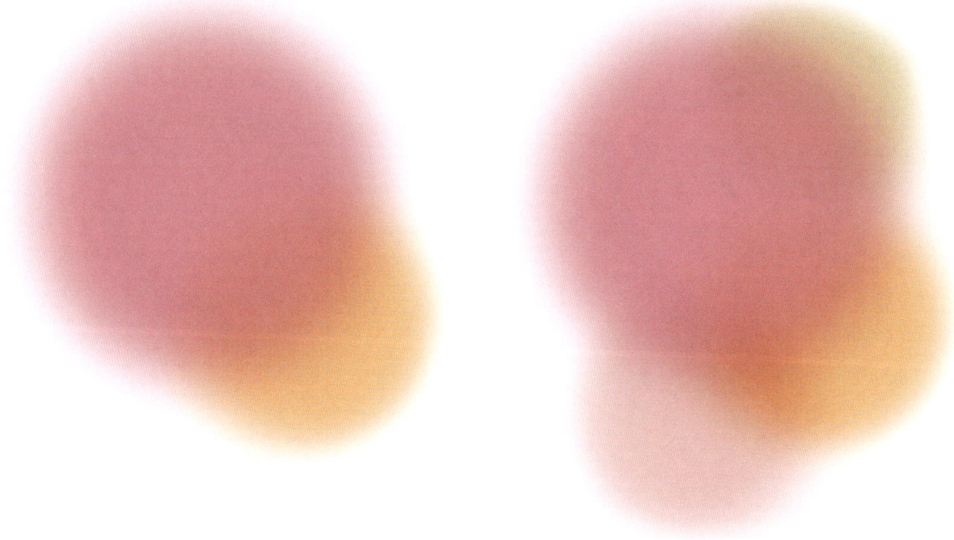

3.

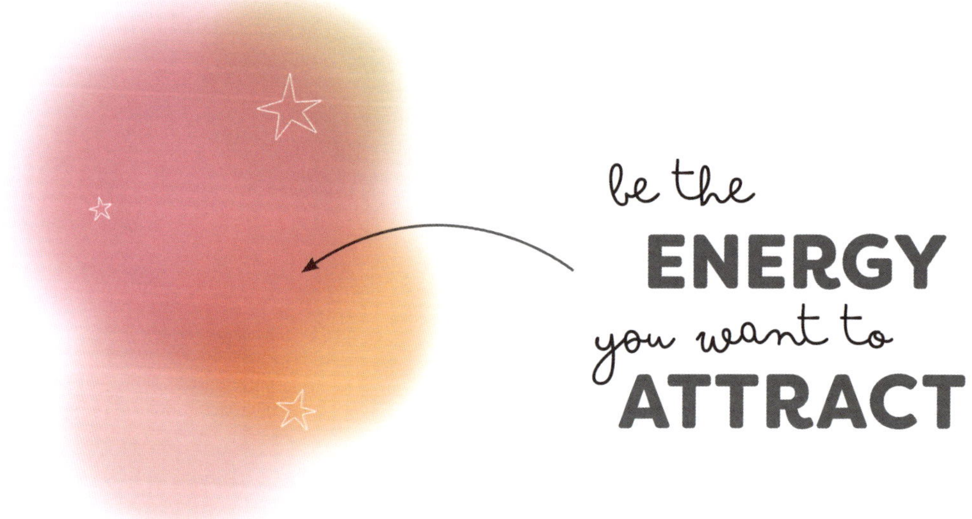

TEXT

Next, I experimented with the text, opting for a mixture of handwritten lettering and a big, bold block capital font. There are so many fonts you could choose from to give you this mix, so you may want to spend some time searching for font styles that you like. Here, I've chosen to use 'Bimbo Pro' for the handwritten lettering and 'Intan' for the block capital letters. I've chosen to use white lettering for this piece as I wanted it to stand out, while also feeling like it was a part of the aura background, as opposed to looking like it was separate and in the foreground.

As the placement of the colours in the background is quite random, I have reflected this in the alignment of the lettering. The script lettering is aligned more to the left side of the page, and the block capital lettering is aligned more to the right. This also helps to create a unity between the background and lettering. Playing around with the alignment of your lettering is very simple to do digitally. Just select the text layer or layers you would like to move, and drag them around the page until you are happy with the placement.

If you are not working digitally, a white marker would be the practical alternative for adding the lettering and stars on top of your background.

ELEMENTS

To create the stars digitally, I chose a pen tool that was roughly the same thickness as the handwritten font, and drew them freehand on a new layer, so they have the same aesthetic as the lettering to help to make this a cohesive piece. Once I had drawn the stars, I experimented with the placement on the page, rotating them and adjusting the sizes until I was happy with the way it sat with the writing and within the artwork as a whole (see page 20 for help with resizing and adjusting your digitally drawn elements).

If you are drawing this piece by hand, I would recommend adding the stars in using the same marker that you are using to write your mantra, as this will help balance the different elements and tie the whole artwork together.

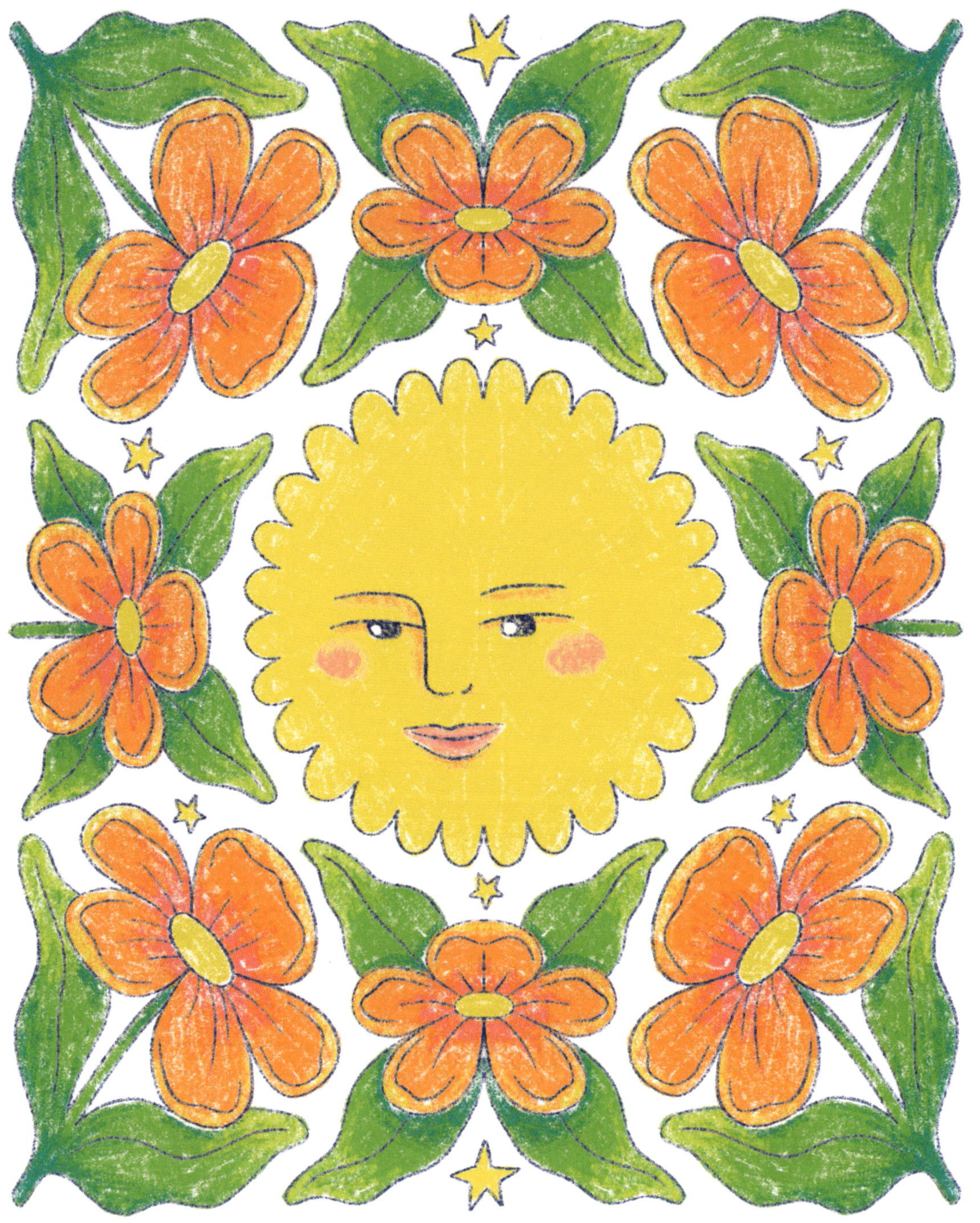

TURN YOUR FACE
TOWARDS THE SUN

TURN YOUR FACE TOWARDS THE SUN

The sun is a metaphor for many inspirational things in life, including light, warmth, happiness and positivity. To turn your face towards the sun means to try and focus on the positives in life, and to let the shadows and negativity fall behind you. Trying to remain focused on the positives in a situation can be challenging, but it's a great practice if you are working towards attracting more positivity into your life.

For this inspirational mantra artwork, we are using the sun and flowers as our main feature. Sunshine and flowers are both things that bring joy to many people, and flowers also naturally grow towards sunlight, so both of these elements work as a great metaphor for this mantra message.

We are using a lot of bright, bold colours in this artwork. These colours will hopefully bring you some happiness while working on this project, and continue to bring joy to you, or whoever you choose to gift your artwork to.

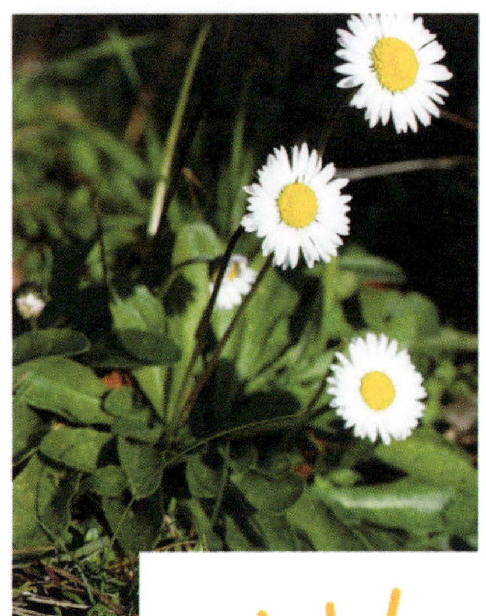

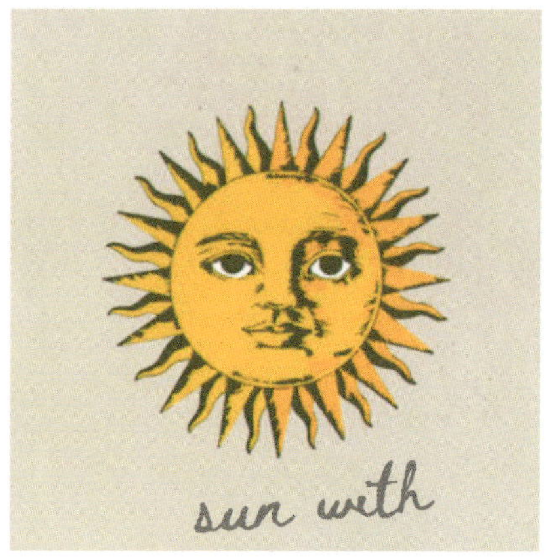

sun with face

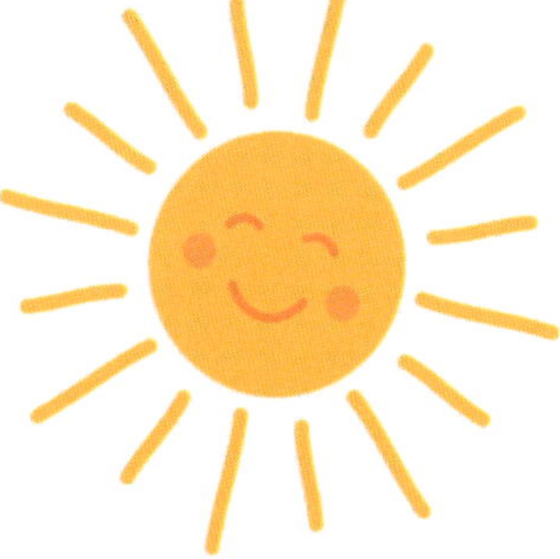

TURN
YOUR
FACE

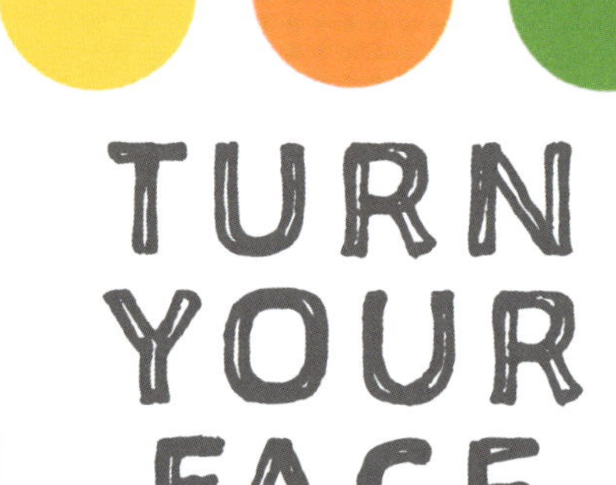

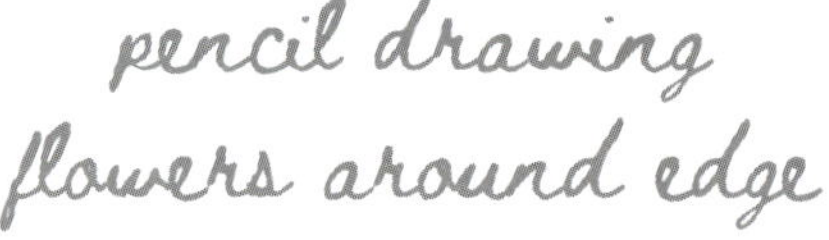

pencil drawing
flowers around edge

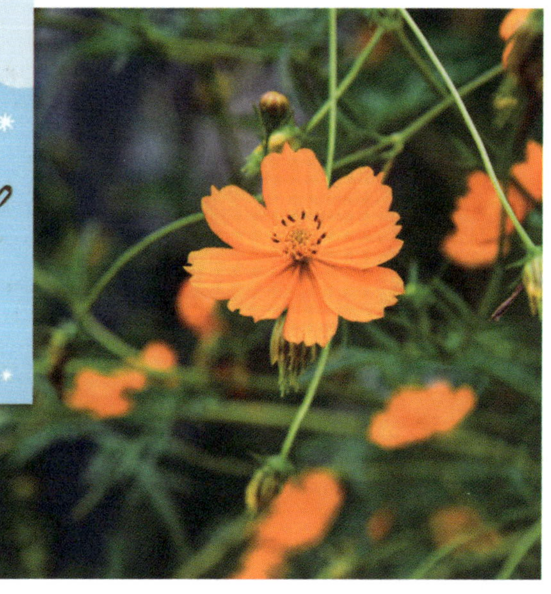

MANTRA MOOD BOARD

Flowers growing towards the sun is a perfect way to illustrate this mantra, as they move in response to the direction of the sunlight. The sun is also at the centre of our solar system, so we'll be using radial symmetry to show the softer elements of the piece revolving around the sun to further emphasize the mantra. We'll also take a closer look at how shading and outlining your illustrative elements can help to add further depth and detail to your pieces, and make them look more refined.

I chose to use bright and bold colours in this artwork, mainly orange and yellow. These colours will help to evoke happiness, warmth and positive energy.

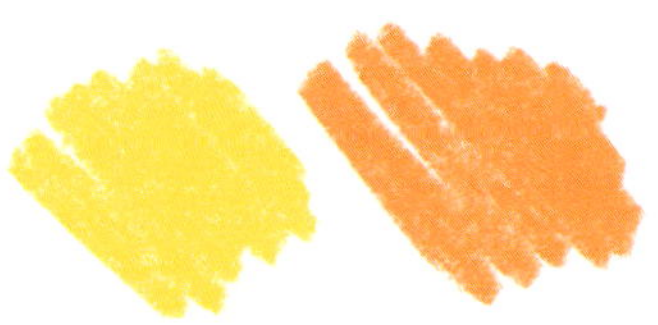

The sun is the main focus of this illustration, so it will be the largest and most detailed motif in the artwork and will be placed in the centre so it stands out.

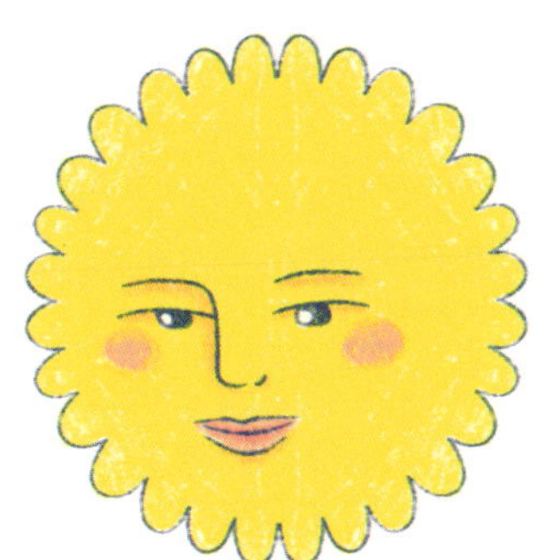

A simpler flower will ensure that the sun is emphasized as the main illustration. The flowers will act as a frame for the sunshine, so I don't want them to be too complex in detail, otherwise they may distract from the sunshine and lettering. I will also use simple stars to symbolize guidance, and to fill any gaps in the piece.

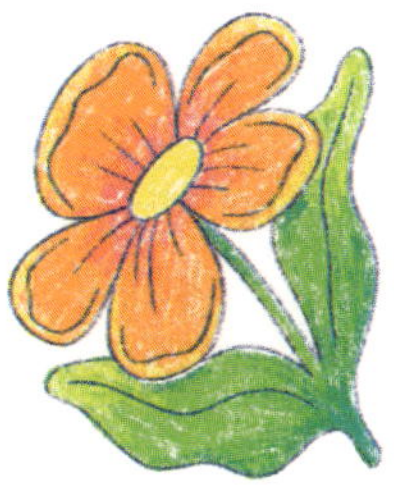

I'll be using capital letters to ensure this mantra text is easy to read. Capitals convey a confident and instructive energy, which will help make this piece more inspiring.

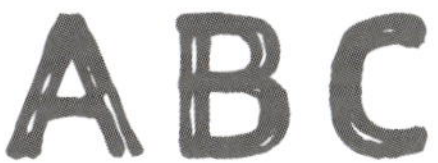

ADDING DETAIL WITH COLOUR AND OUTLINES

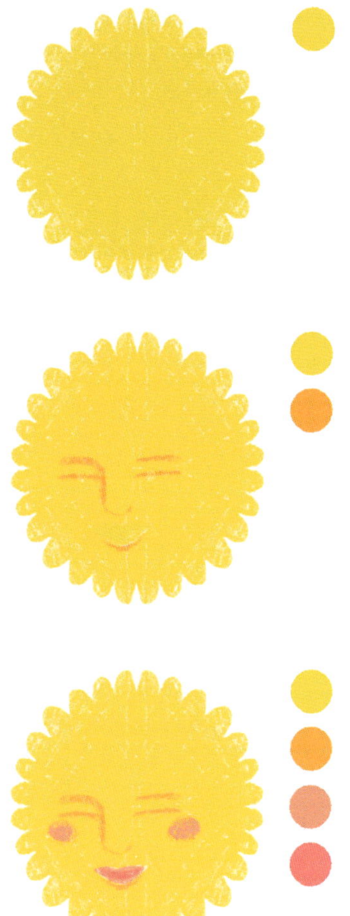

Using a range of colours is a great way to add detail to an illustration. Here, only small amounts of colour have been added with each layer, but each colour helps to add depth to the illustration.

ADDING DEPTH WITH LIGHTER AND DARKER COLOURS

When figuring out where to add light and shade, it's helpful to imagine a light source shining on the object from a particular direction, and the highlights and shadows that would be created by this. With this sunshine, for example, you can imagine that the light source is coming from the top left corner and shining across the face. This will create shadows under the eyebrows, eyes, nose and mouth. I haven't added highlights here, as this drawing style is not very realistic. However, I have added rosy cheeks and red lips to highlight those features.

ADDING OUTLINES FOR EMPHASIS

Outlining certain elements of your illustrations can also help to add depth and boldness to your piece. You may choose to outline some elements (to make them more prominent) and not others, so that they are less prominent. You can also experiment, using different colours for outlining your pieces, and use different medias (like a black fine liner).

Whether you choose to add an outline or not may be different with every illustration, but in this example, you can see that adding an outline helps to emphasize the sun's facial features. Not adding an outline also gives the illustration a much softer feel, so you may want to experiment with this effect when drawing mantras to evoke different emotions.

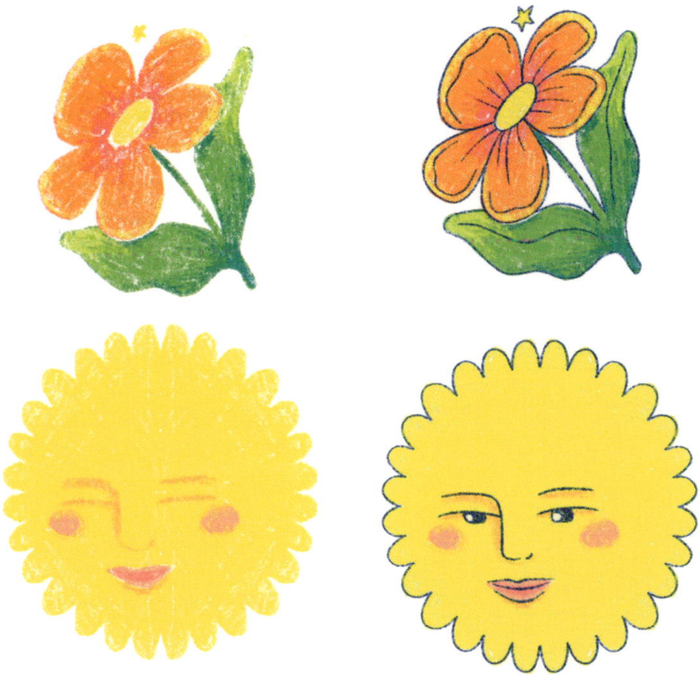

COMPOSITION

To create my mantra, I used Photoshop, following the steps on pages 16-23 to prepare for my project. The practical media alternative for this artwork would be coloured pencil, or you could experiment with using crayon or oil pastels for the colour and pencil or liner for the outlines and lettering.

ELEMENTS

As the sun was to be the focal point of this artwork, I used flowers to surround it, as they grow towards the sun in nature. I used quadrant symmetry in this piece to simplify the task of organizing my flowers around the sunshine (see steps on page 53).

When drawing this piece digitally, I drew the linework first and then added the colours in layers below this linework. I started with blocking out the base colours of each element, then added in the highlight and shadows.

The drawing style for this artwork is looser than some of the previous designs. As you can see, there are some gaps between the pencil strokes and I haven't been so careful with keeping the colour solid. Keep this in mind when choosing the type of media you would like to use, as you'll want to choose something that creates this same effect.

If you are drawing this piece using a practical alternative, you'll need to use a ruler and light pencil to divide your paper into four sections. Then, using the steps detailed on page 53, draw your linework for one of the quadrants, then use tracing paper to fill in the other three quadrants.

Once this is done, use your practical medium to add colour to your piece. You'll want to build up the layers from your base colours, just as you would do if you were drawing digitally. Once you are satisfied with your colour, go over your linework with either a dark pencil or fine liner pen to highlight the detail in the elements.

TEXT

I used a simple font – 'Fenwick' – that would not overwhelm the artwork as a whole.

If you are creating your artwork using the practical media alternative, handwriting your mantra in clear, capital letters will have the same effect.

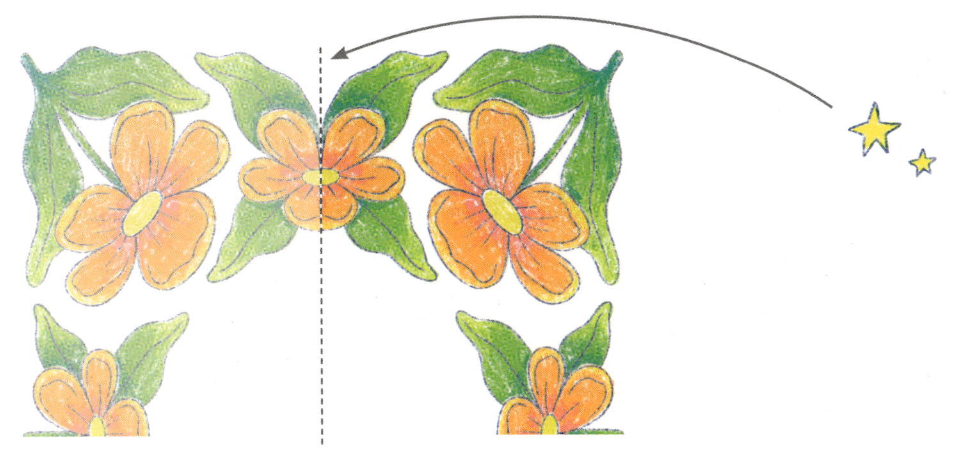

TURN YOUR FACE

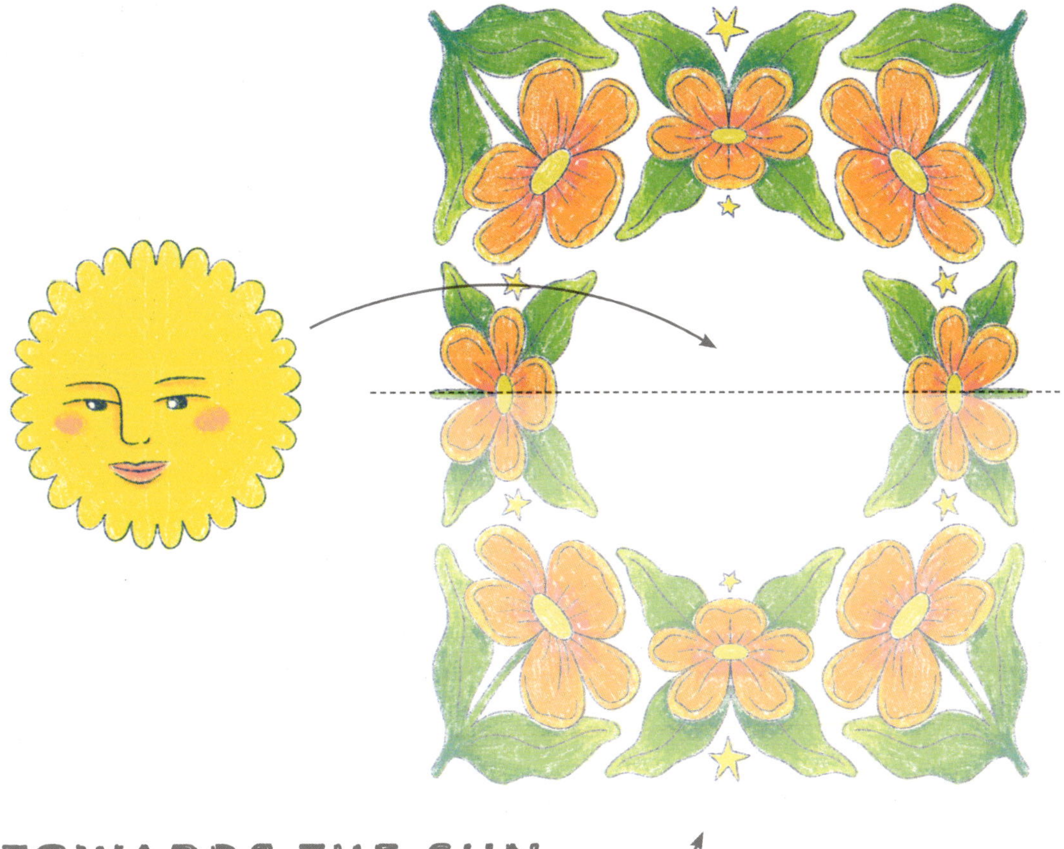

TOWARDS THE SUN

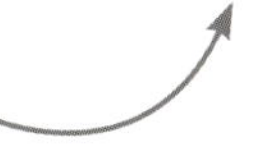

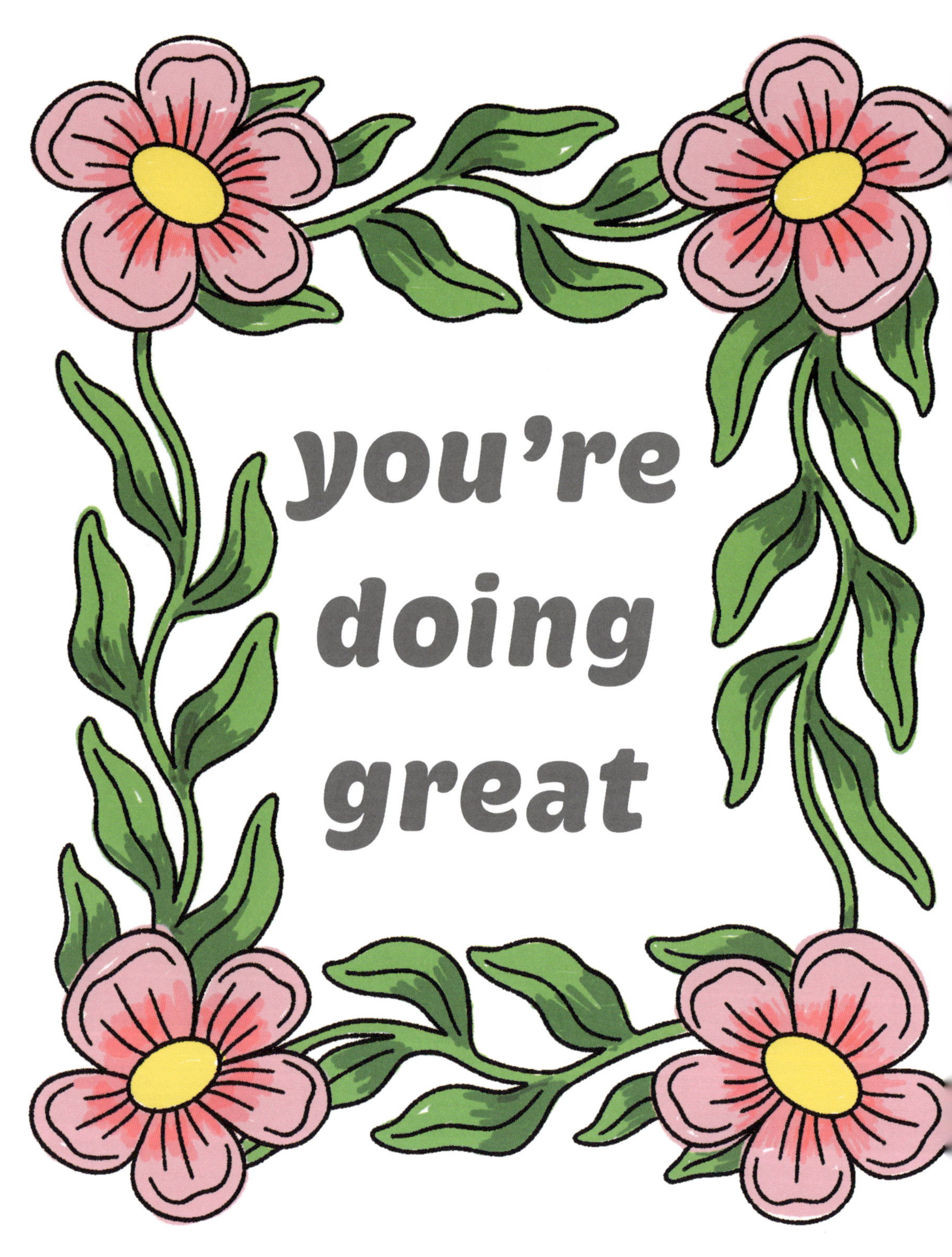
you're
doing
great

YOU'RE DOING GREAT

We all need some encouragement now and then, whether we're working on a specific project, working towards a particular goal or just getting through a challenging day. Taking the time to acknowledge and appreciate your own efforts with this uplifting mantra is a small but powerful way to boost confidence and motivation.

Many people find that positive self-talk does not come naturally to them and, as with forming any habit, it takes time and practice before it begins to feel more natural. Once you have created your artwork in this project, I encourage you to put it somewhere where it is visible to you every day, and use it as a reminder that you're doing great.

In this project, we are going to look into the technique of creating frames for your text using illustrative motifs. In this example, we are using flowers to make our frame, as flowers are commonly used as a gift to show appreciation. Framing your lettering is a simple but effective technique to elevate the message you want to send and turn it into artwork that you or whoever you are gifting it to will want to have on the wall.

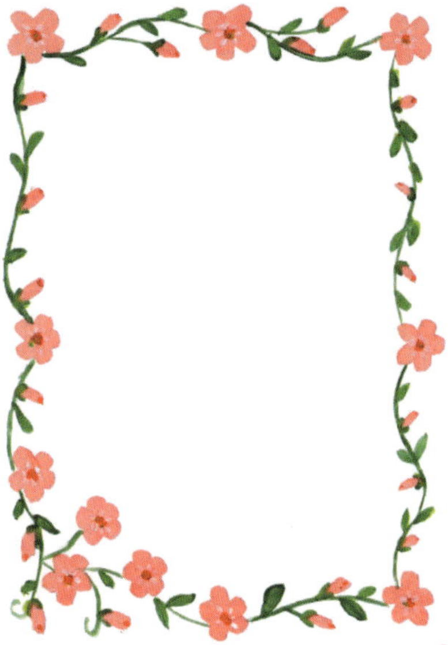

great

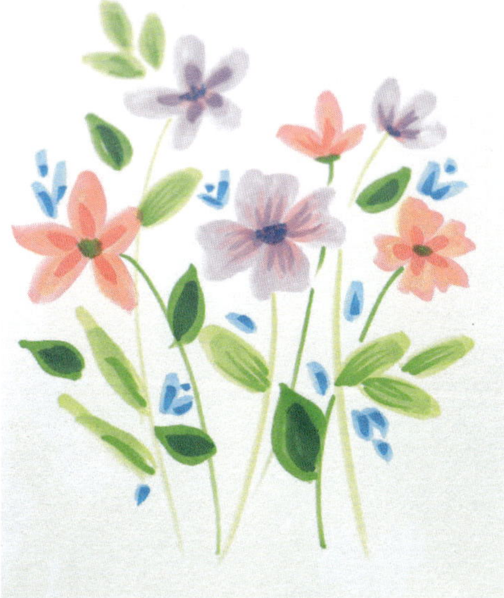

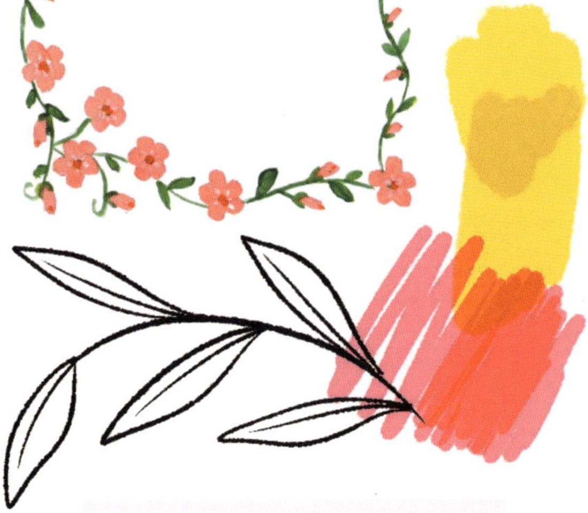

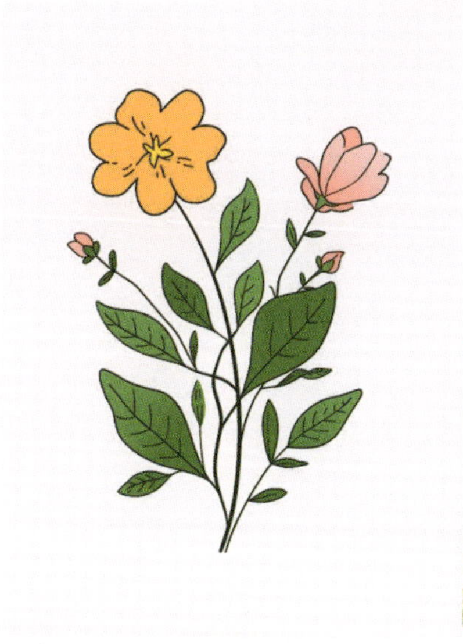

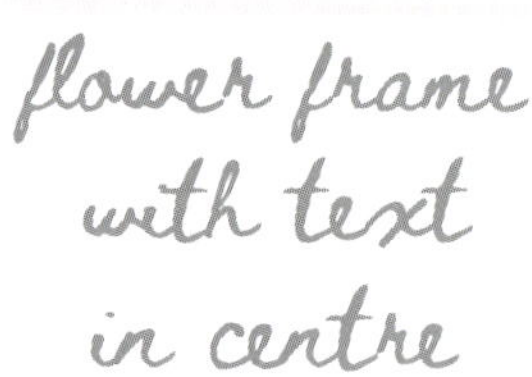

flower frame
with text
in centre

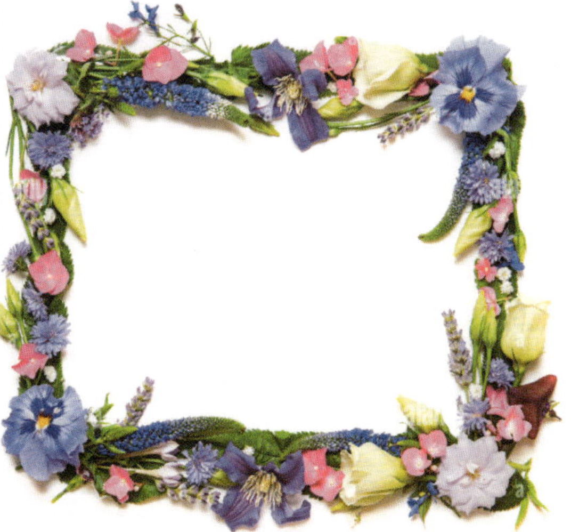

MANTRA MOOD BOARD

For this mantra artwork, we are going to experiment with using framing as a tool for emphasizing our illustration and mantra message.

I have chosen to use pink as the predominant colour of the flowers in this piece as pink symbolizes love, nurturing and compassion, which perfectly ties in to the message of this mantra. I will be using a more realistic colour palette here, with green leaves, pink petals and a yellow centre.

I have chosen to use a font that is bold and italic so it will stand out among the illustrative elements. This font is quite minimal in style so it will complement the minimal amount of detail in the illustration.

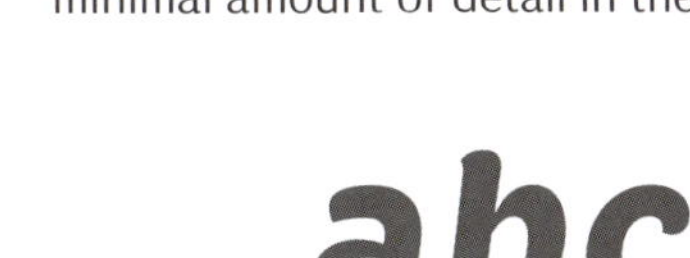

I will be using flowers as the main motif in this illustration, as they are a symbol of growth and love, which matches the message of our mantra. I'll also be using a frame to connect the flowers together, to symbolize supporting each other through growth.

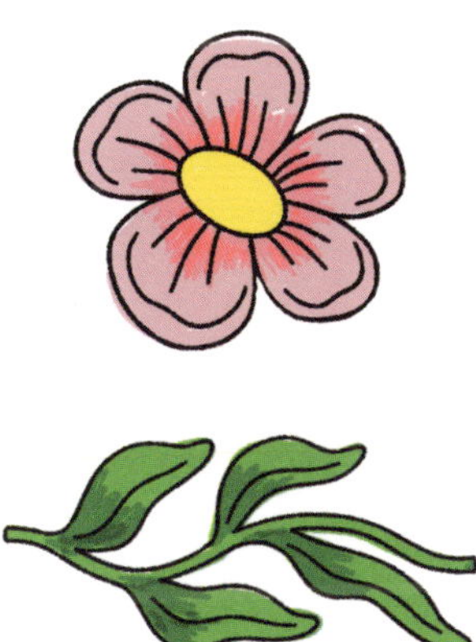

USING FRAMES

Framing is a simple technique that will create a focal point for your artwork. A frame is a great option when you want the lettering to be the main focus of the artwork, as it immediately draws the eye to whatever's in the centre. Flowers are a classic motif for framing, but you can use any element you choose.

RECTANGULAR FRAMES

A rectangular or square frame is a good option if you have a longer message or want to use large letters, as it will leave more space inside the frame for your lettering.

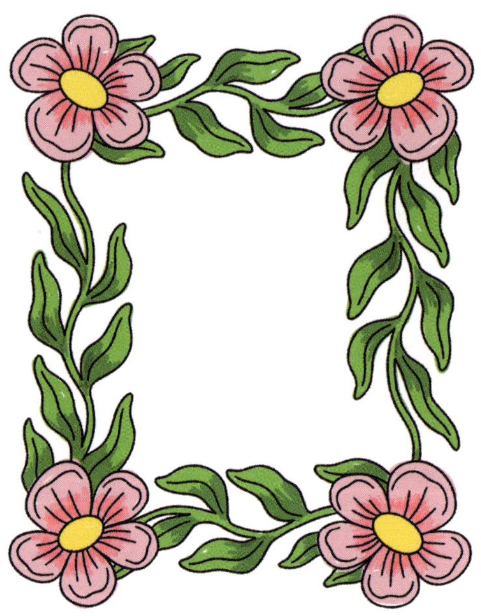

How to Create

If you are creating a frame using Photoshop, create your frame shape using the rectangular 'Shape' tool in one layer to use as a guide. Then, create another layer for your illustrations.

You can either draw freely to create your frame so it doesn't have any symmetry to it, or you could draw a small section, then duplicate it by right-clicking on the layer in the 'Layers' panel, clicking 'Duplicate Layer', then joining it to the end of the initial section to create a repeating pattern. You may have to flip it horizontally or vertically, especially if you are looking to achieve a symmetrical look (see pages 52–53). Refer back to the Photoshop guide at the start of this book if you need help with any of these steps.

To draw your frame by hand, lightly draw your guide in pencil on a piece of paper (to be erased later). Use a ruler if you want it to be precise. Once you are happy with your guide, you can make a start decorating your frame. As with the digital description, you can just freely fill the frame without any symmetry, or you could use tracing paper to utilize symmetry (see page 53) in order to create the same effect that you see in the example artwork.

Once you have sketched out your frame, go ahead with colouring it in using the medium of your choice. You can then erase what you can of the frame outline.

CIRCULAR FRAMES

A circular frame is a good choice for a
shorter message, or something like initials or
one letter.

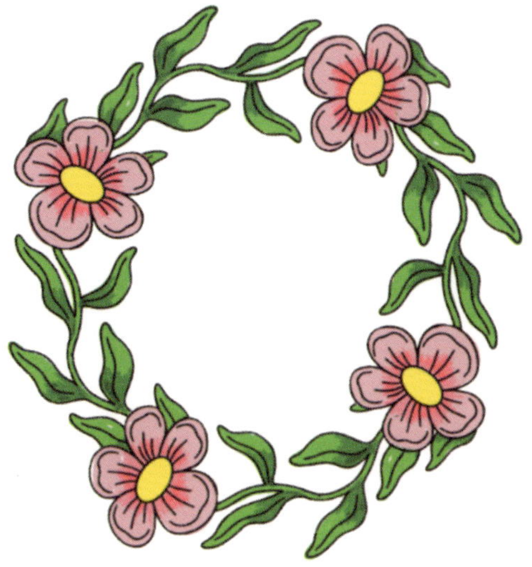

How to Create

If you are creating a frame using Photoshop,
make your frame shape using the 'Ellipse'
tool in one layer to use as a guide. Then,
create another layer for your illustrations.

As with the rectangular frame, you can either
draw freely to create your frame so it doesn't
have any symmetry to it, or you could draw
a small section, duplicate it by right-clicking
on the layer in the 'Layers' panel, then click
'Duplicate Layer' and join it to the end of the
initial section to create a repeating pattern.
You may need to also rotate it, especially
if you are looking to achieve a symmetrical
look. Refer back to the Photoshop guide at
the start of this book for if you need help
with any of these steps.

On a piece of paper, lightly draw your guide
in pencil. Use a compass or small plate if
you want it to be precise. Once you are
happy with your guide, you can make a
start on your frame. You can freely fill the
frame without any symmetry, or you can
use tracing paper to utilize symmetry in
order to create the same effect that you
see in the example artwork.

Once you have sketched out your frame,
go ahead with colouring it in using the
medium of your choice. You can then erase
what you can of the frame outline.

COMPOSITION

Once you have decided on your colour palette, elements you would like to include in your mantra artwork, and the type of frame you would like to use, you can begin to assemble your artwork.

To create my mantra, I used Photoshop following the steps on pages 16–23 to prepare for my project. The practical media alternative for this artwork would be coloured markers, however, you could also use coloured pencil or acrylic paint, and a liner for the outline detail and lettering.

ELEMENTS

I used flowers in this mantra artwork, as the idea of giving flowers with a message is a common way to make someone feel loved and cared for. I drew one outlined flower and leaf section in one layer, then coloured it in digitally on a separate layer underneath. I then used the steps on pages 86–87 to create a symmetrical frame.

If you are drawing by hand, I recommend lightly sketching out your flower and leaf section, colouring it, then outlining your drawing with a clean line so that the line details are clear.

TEXT

I chose to use a clean font (Gill Sans) in the illustration, as the style of illustration used in the frame is quite simple. However, to make the lettering stand out in the artwork, I made it bold and italic, and also increased the tracking and leading between the letters and words so that it has more impact.

If you are writing your lettering by hand, I recommend lightly writing it in pencil first so that you get your spacing correct, then you can either use a thick pen, or outline your letters and colour them in black.

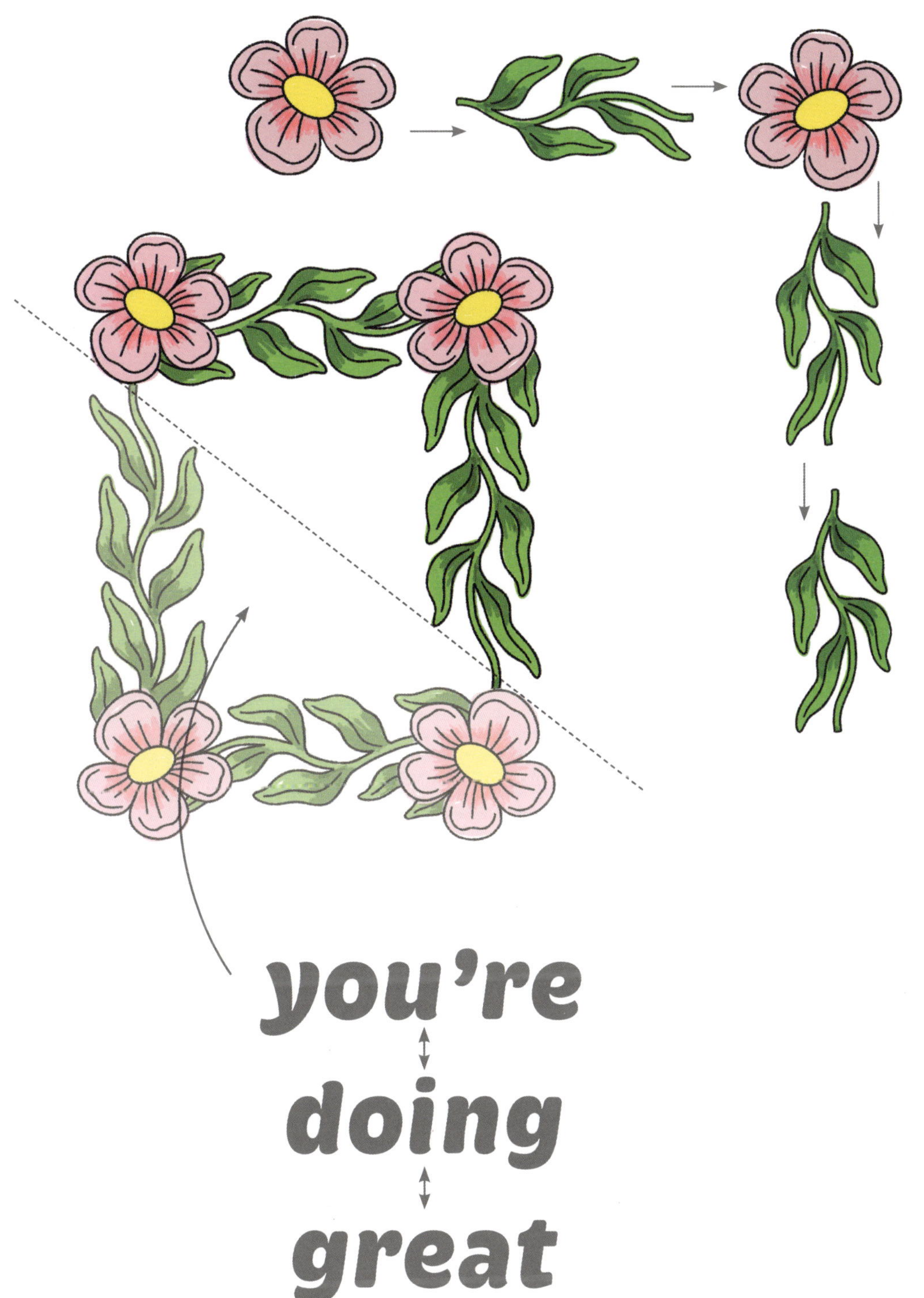

you're
doing
great

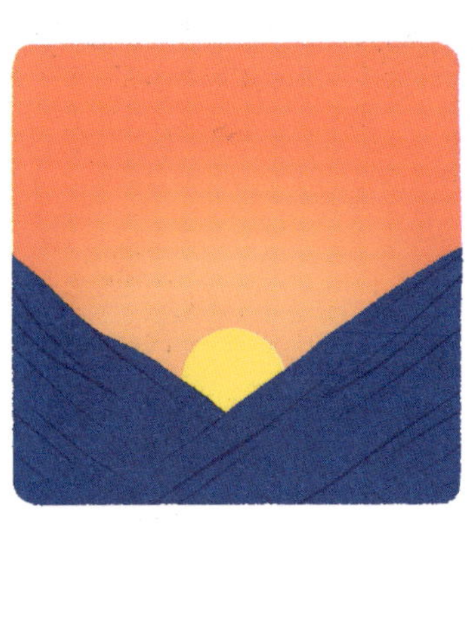 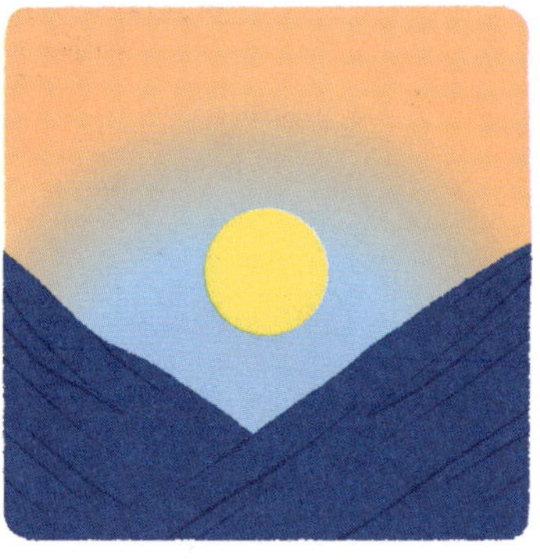 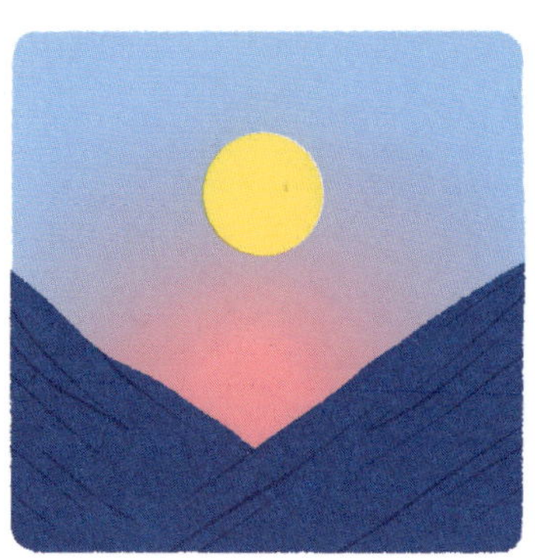

BETTER

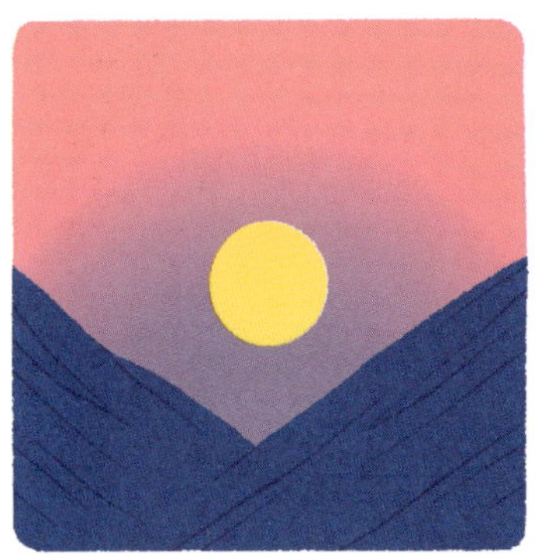 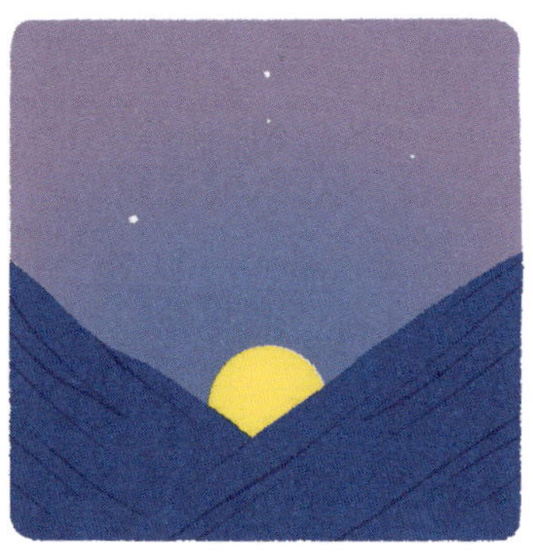 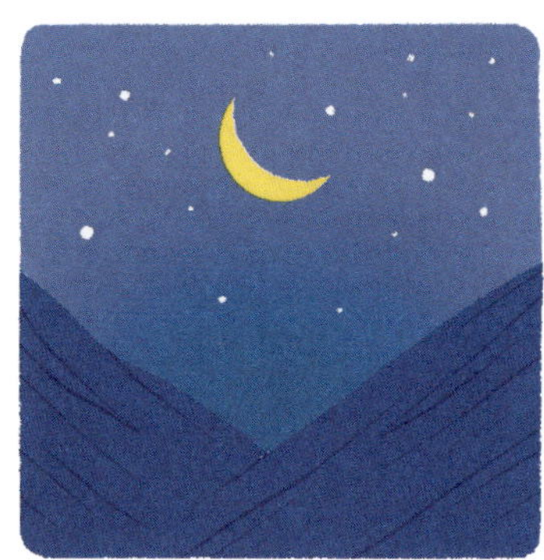

DAYS

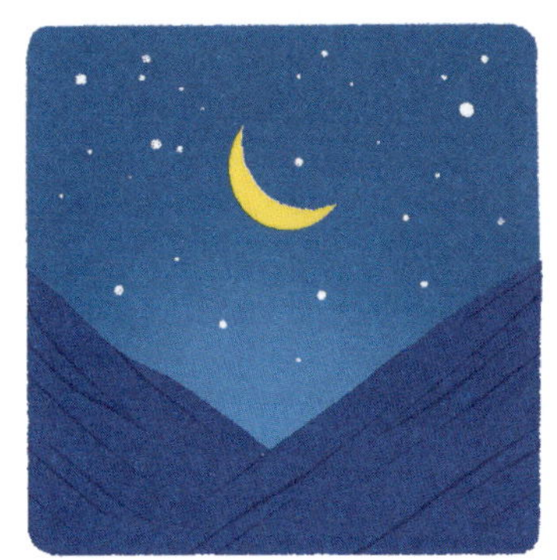 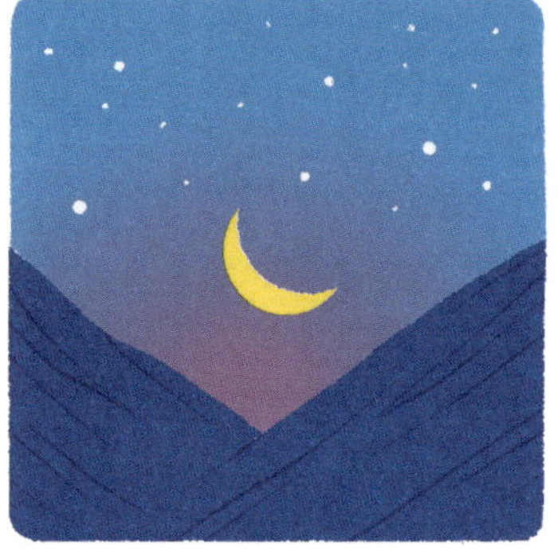 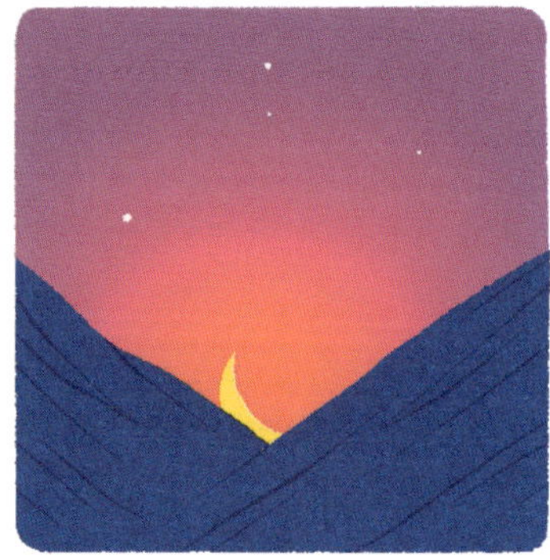

AHEAD

BETTER DAYS AHEAD

We all have bad days now and then, and when things build up, it's easy to feel overwhelmed. Sometimes it feels as though we are completely out of control in challenging situations, but if you are able to spend some time at the end of each day to allow yourself to decompress and think about any small actions you can take to make tomorrow a better day, you can take steps to stop a bad day from becoming a bad week.

In this chapter, we are going to look at using illustration to tell a story through the use of storyboard layouts. We will explore how we can observe the motion of an object, break it down into simple movements and translate that into our drawing using processes including sketching and tracing.

We are using the changing sky to illustrate the process of the day turning into night, and with the rainbow of colours in our colour palette, I hope this artwork will uplift you or whoever you choose to gift it to as a reminder that better days are coming.

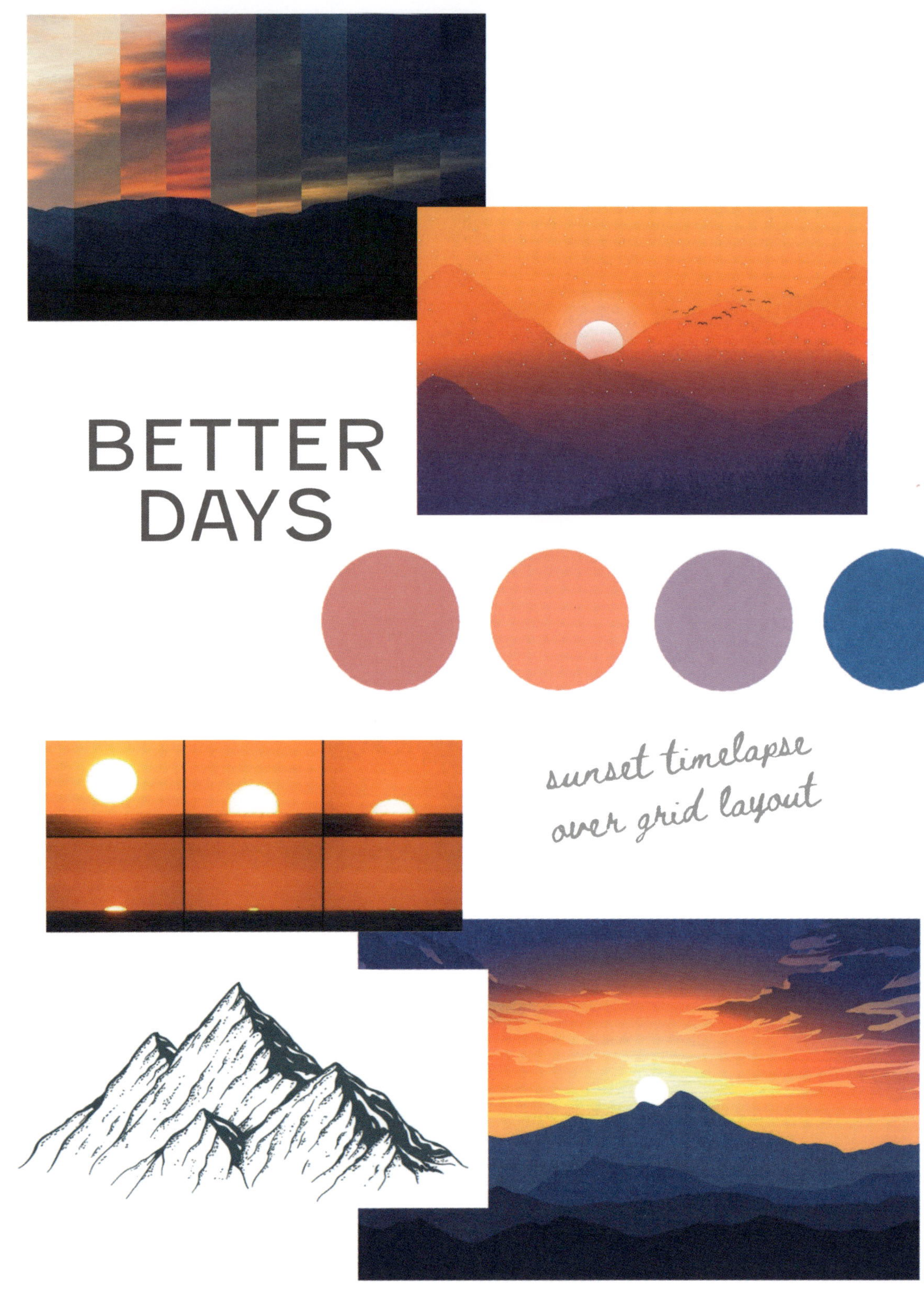

BETTER
DAYS
sunset timelapse
over grid layout

MANTRA MOOD BOARD

Using this storyboard-style layout is a useful technique for showing a process happening, as you can show a different part of the process in each frame. This piece is showing the sky changing over one day, from sunrise to sunset, to emphasize the message that a new day is just around the corner.

I'll be using a variety of sunset- and sunrise-inspired shades in a gradient form to help illustrate the passing of time as the sun and moon rise and set.

We are using a mountain landscape as the background for this artwork – the mountain will stay exactly the same in each frame to show that we are looking at the same view, but as we want to illustrate a day passing in this illustration, we are going to include three things that will help us to do that.

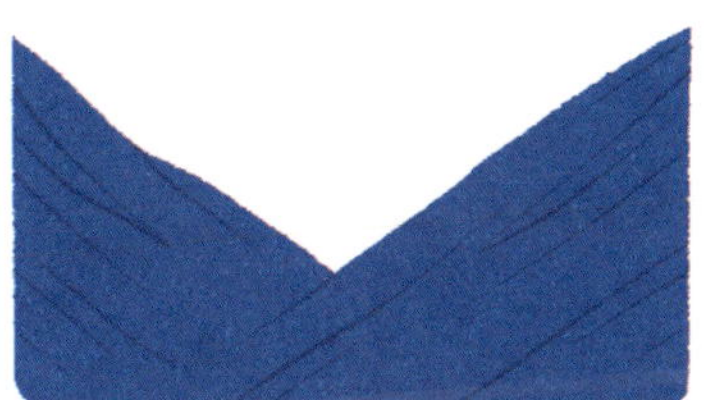

I'll be drawing the sun, moon and stars for my elements to help tell my story.

As this illustration is going to be a timelapse layout, I'll add the text in below the frames so that it is on a blank background and clear to read. The lettering is quite small in scale as it has to fit between the lines in the artwork, so capital letters will help the message to be seen amongst the artwork.

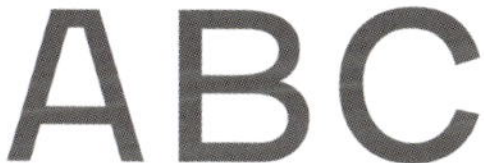

HOW TO USE GRIDS

Using a grid layout in your artwork is a useful tool for telling a story or showing a process happening over time. You can use more frames in your grid if you want to show a process in more detail, or to show a longer process taking place, such as time passing over a day. Here, we'll look at creating a nine-square grid.

DRAWING A GRID DIGITALLY

1. Set up your canvas on Photoshop using the steps on pages 16–17. For this project, I advise using the canvas size A4, which is 210mm x 297mm (8¼in x 11¾in).

2. Your squares need to be 5cm x 5cm (2in x 2in). Using the 'Rectangle' tool on the left-hand tool bar, click on your canvas to bring up the 'Create Rectangle' window that will allow you to put your dimensions in.

3. Once created, the square will appear on your canvas and you can change the colour and line thickness using the top toolbar (I recommend 10 px for your line weight). Next, using the 'Selection' tool, click on your square and move it to the centre of your canvas. It should snap into place once you move it to the centre.

4. Copy and paste this square twice to create, then start by completing the middle row, dragging the squares into place. Remember to leave roughly a 1-cm (½-in) gap between the squares.

5. Once the middle row is complete, you can use the 'Selection' tool to select the whole row and copy and paste this to create the row above. You'll need to leave roughly a 2-cm (¾-in) gap between the rows to have space for your text.

6. Finally, copy and paste your row once more and drag it to create the final row below.

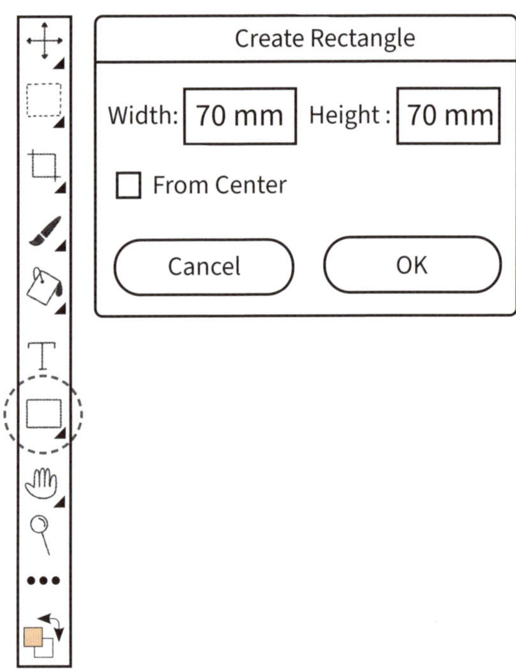

DRAWING A GRID BY HAND

We're going to run through an example of how to measure out a nine-square grid by hand. You will need a piece of gridded paper, a piece of A4 paper, a pencil and a 30-cm (12-in) ruler.

1. Place your gridded paper underneath your drawing paper. You need to be able to see the grid through the paper, so you may need to use a light box or hold your paper up to a window to let the light through.

2. To draw your grid, your squares will need to be 5cm x 5cm (2in x 2in). Gridded paper squares are usually 5mm x 5mm (¼in x ¼in), so this will easily allow you to work out the sizes of your squares for your artwork. Begin by locating the centre of your paper. Then, using your 5-mm (¼-in) grid guide, measure and mark 10 squares horizontally and 10 squares vertically around your central point on the page. This will be your first square.

3. Next, draw two squares either side of your middle one, including a 1-cm (½-in) gap on either side (two squares horizontally, and two squares vertically).

4. You'll need to add a 2-cm (¾-in) gap (four squares) between the middle row and the ones above and below, as you need to leave space for your lettering. Once you've marked this, you can draw in the rows above and below using the same process used for the middle row.

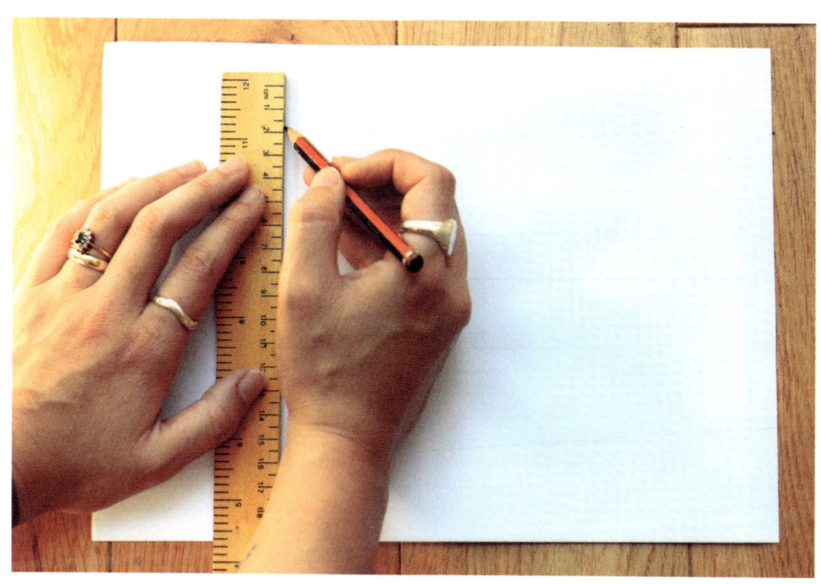

COMPOSITION

I used Photoshop for this piece following the steps on pages 16–23 to prepare for my project. The practical media alternative for this artwork would be to create a mixed media artwork. As you need to create a gradient background, chalk pastels or watercolour paint would be good options. Fine liners or coloured pencil would be the option for the linework and mantra lettering.

BACKGROUND

To start, I created a nine-square grid storyboard to place each of my mini-scenes in (see pages 94–95). I then created gradients for each of the nine scene squares (see page 68–69 for help creating gradients), remembering to leave space to add in the mountains under the sky.

To use a practical medium to create this background, use the steps on page 95.

ELEMENTS

This artwork depicts the changing sky over a mountain landscape, and the mountain stays the same across the nine frames. In frames 1–5, I depict the sun rising into the middle of the landscape from behind the mountain and back down, and in frames 6–9, the moon sets down from the middle of the frame back behind the mountain.

When drawing the mountains, sun and moon, I kept them to the same shape and colour. In order to keep them the same when drawing digitally, I drew them in frame 1, and then copy and pasted them to use into my other frames, repositioning the sun and moon in each frame (but leaving the mountain in place). Finally, I added some stars to frames 6–9.

If you are drawing by hand, you could use the tracing method explained on page 53 to draw your mountain in frame 1 and then use your tracing paper to copy it onto your other frames. You can add the stars using a white pen at the end.

TEXT

As there is a lot going on in the illustrated part of this mantra artwork, I chose to use a simple font (called 'Fenwick') for my mantra. I positioned one word beneath each row of three squares to flow with the forward-moving theme of the story.

If you are drawing your mantra artwork by hand, hand-writing in capitals will have the same effect as using the typed font used here.

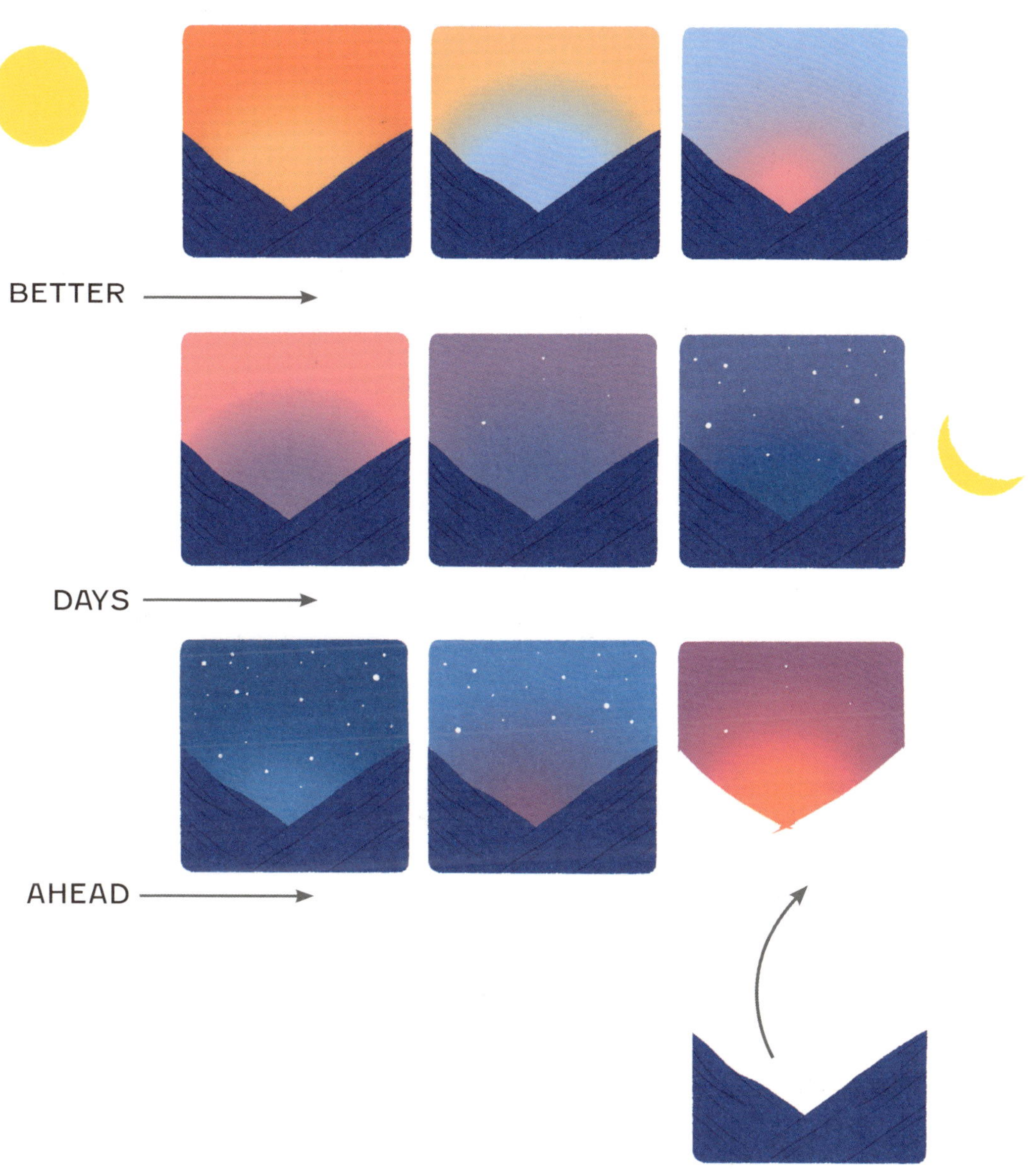

BETTER
DAYS
AHEAD

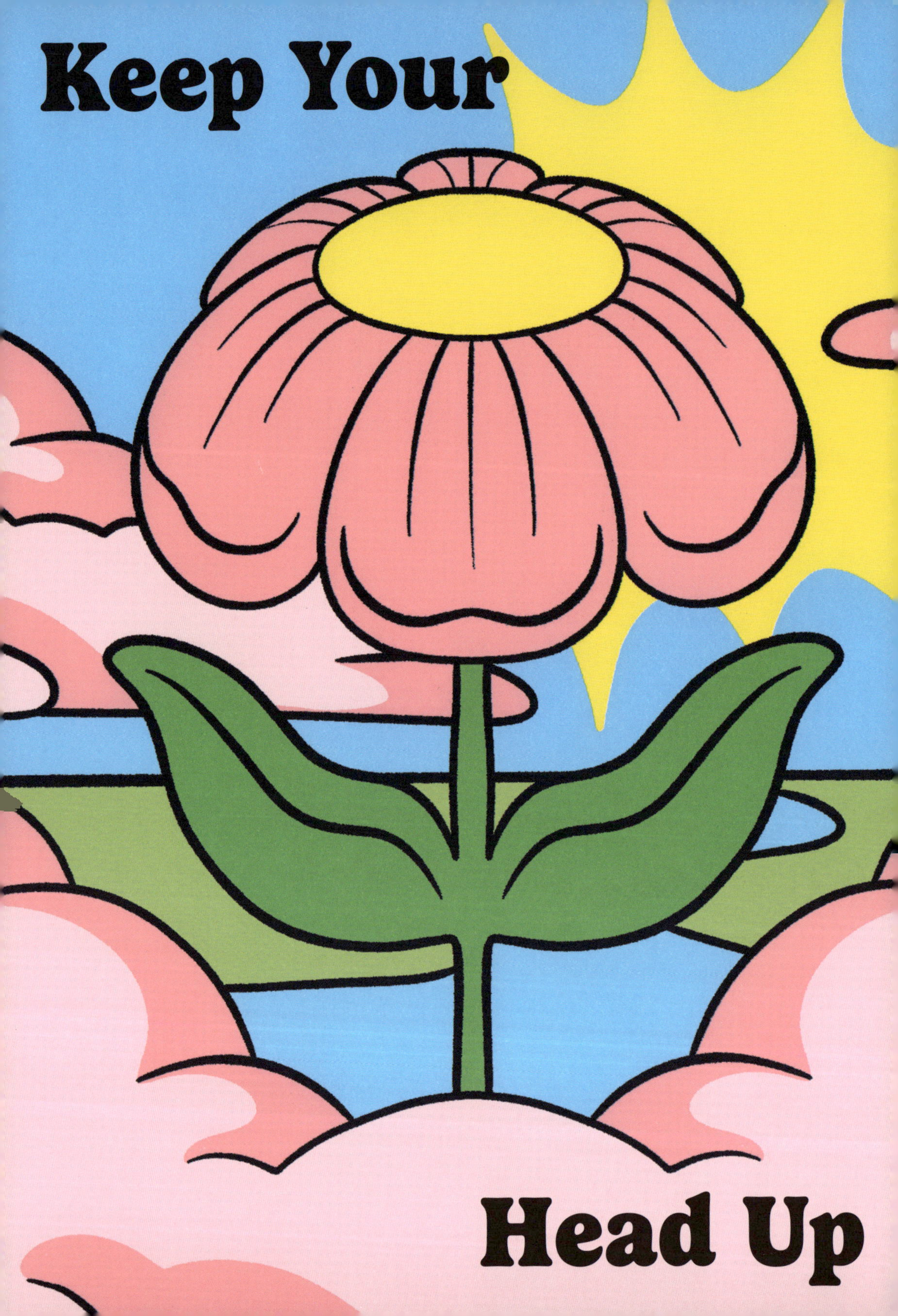

Keep Your
Head Up

KEEP YOUR HEAD UP

Keeping your head up means being proud of yourself. Whether you use this as a general mantra to remind yourself to be proud of where you are at in your life, or as a reminder to be resilient in the more challenging moments, this simple mantra can help to uplift you when you need it.

Taking the time to acknowledge your achievements and growth can contribute to a higher sense of self-worth, and the positive effects of this can spread into many areas of our lives. Keeping your head up, valuing your growth, and using this to uplift and motivate you will help you to achieve your goals, big or small.

In this chapter, we are going to use the image of a flower growing high above the clouds and land below as a metaphor for our mantra. Inspired by retro art styles, we are going to be using bright colours and bold shapes to make this artwork vibrant and eye-catching so you'll be reminded of this uplifting mantra message whenever you see it.

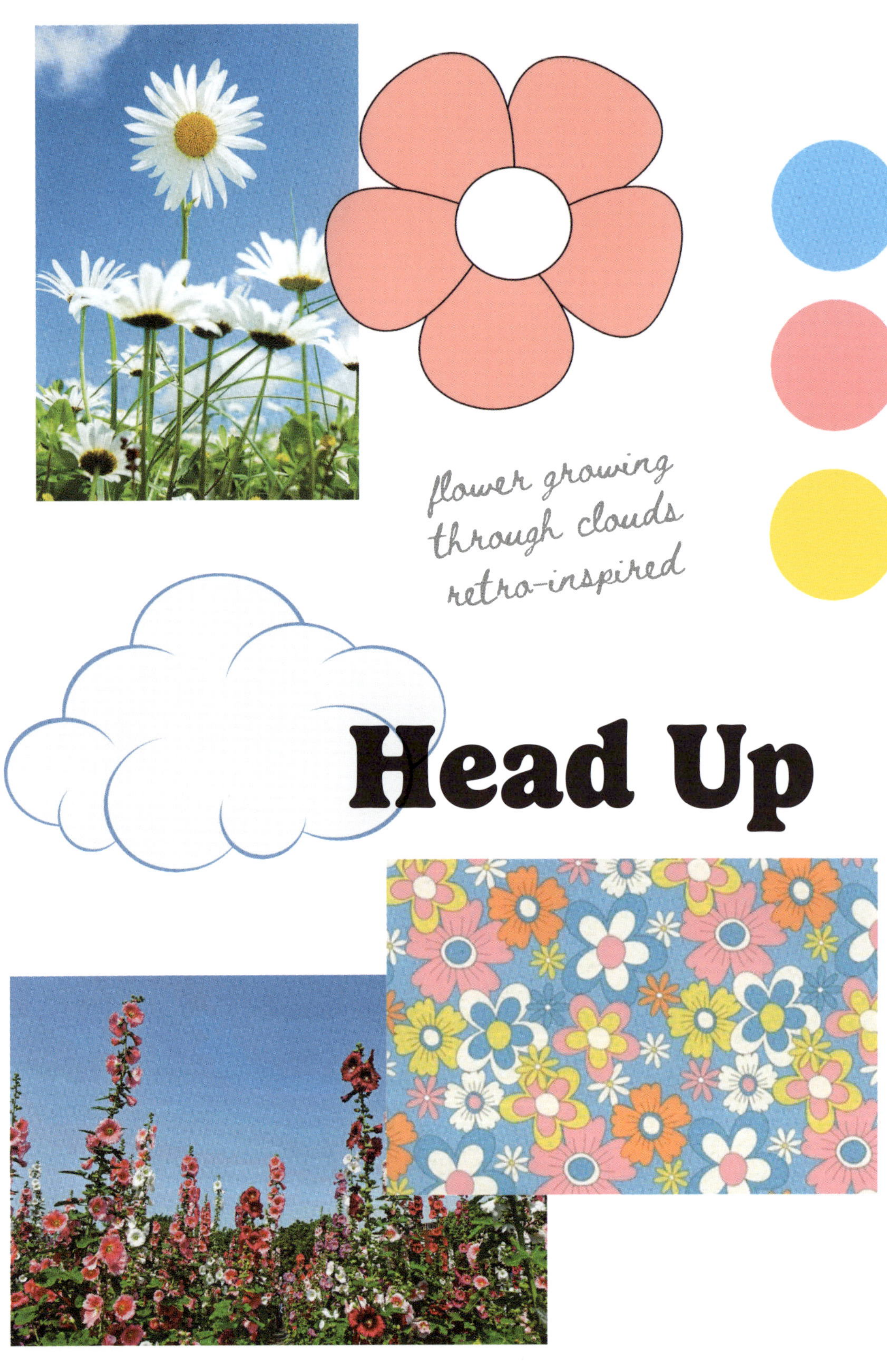

flower growing
through clouds
retro-inspired

Head Up

MANTRA MOOD BOARD

This mantra illustration is based upon the image of a flower growing above the clouds towards the sunshine, which is an ideal image to help you convey the message 'keep your head up'. While the imagery you will be using for this project is quite specific, we'll also be looking more into different art styles. I'll be looking to retro art to inform my piece, but I encourage you to play around with different genres to suit your own preferences.

The colour palette for this artwork is a saturated version of the colours you might expect to find on a flower, as the style of this piece draws inspiration from retro influences, which use a lot of bold, eye-catching colours.

A flower is going to be the main focus of this artwork, and I'll be drawing it in the centre of the piece and at a large scale. The centre of the flower will be the highest point, and the petals will be pulled downwards to show how fast the flower is growing.

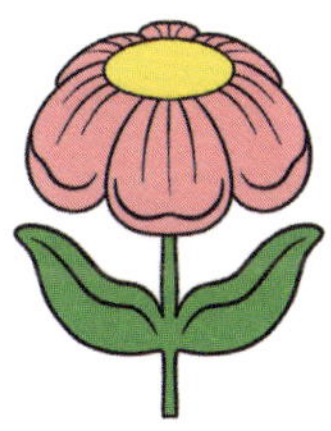

A simple sun in the background will show that the flower is growing up towards it, and some clouds surrounding the flower will help to show how high the flower is growing. I will put most of the cloud towards the base of the flower and the bottom of the page to show that the flower has grown above the cloud line and the landscape below.

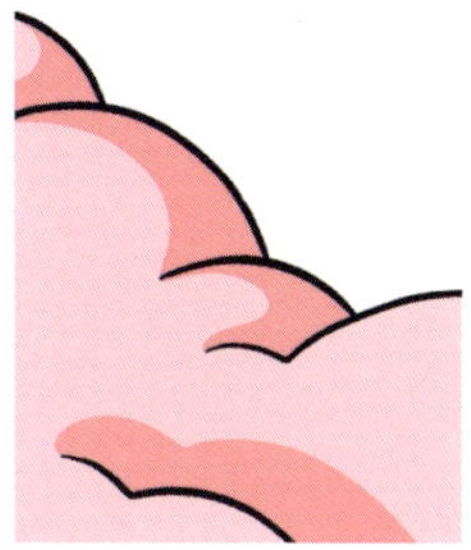

For the lettering, I want something bold so it's visible against the busy background, and I'll keep the lettering black so it doesn't over-complicate the piece. This particular artwork has more of a retro design influence, so I will also be using a lettering style that will suit this aesthetic.

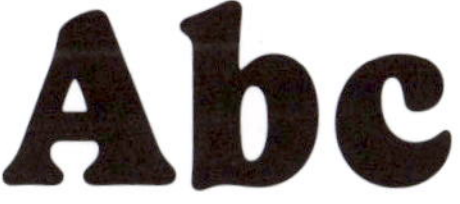

TAKING INSPIRATION FROM ART MOVEMENTS

The illustrative elements used in the example artwork are inspired by the retro design styles of the 70s. If you look at reference images from the design styles of this era, you can see a lot of bright colours and clean lines are used, which you can also see featured in the example artwork. In this section we are going to take a look at a few different art styles, identify the defining characteristics of each style, and see how you can experiment with adding these characteristics into your artwork to create different effects or moods.

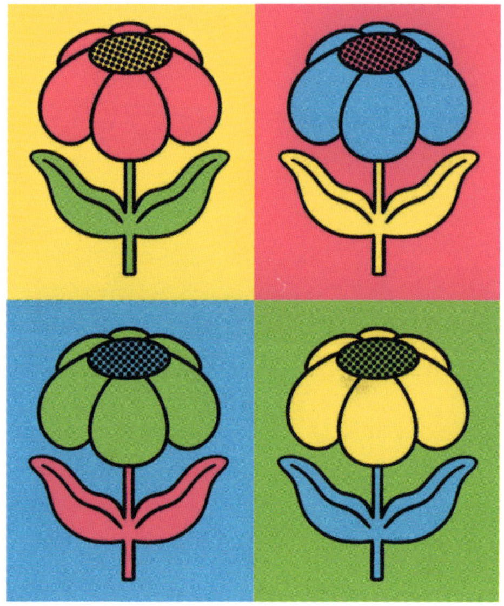

POP ART

Pop Art was a movement that gained popularity in the 1960s. If you take a look at some Pop Art examples, you will see that the key characteristics include bright and bold colours, defined shapes and repetition. The flower in this example already has a defined outline that makes the shape clear to the viewer, but if we adjust the colour palette and incorporate the dot pattern and repetition (which is a very distinctive feature of Pop Art), the effect is very different.

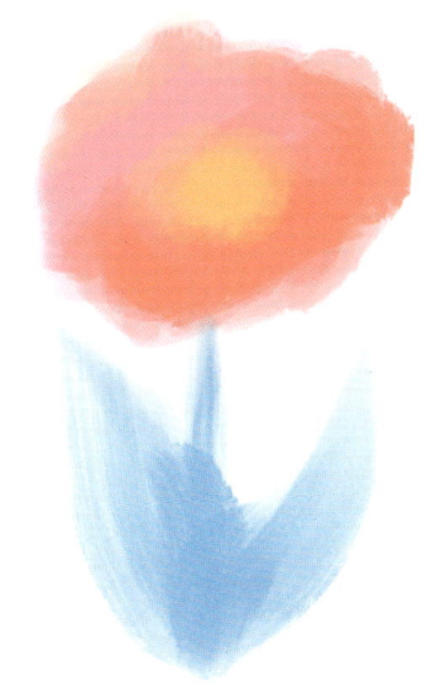

ABSTRACT ART

Abstract art is art that doesn't attempt to portray an accurate depiction of reality. It can be more subjective and open to interpretation by the viewer. When trying to draw this flower in a more abstract style, I have used the same colour for the petals but drawn them with much looser brushstrokes to try and convey more of the movement of the flower. I also did not include an outline to give the flower a free-er feel.

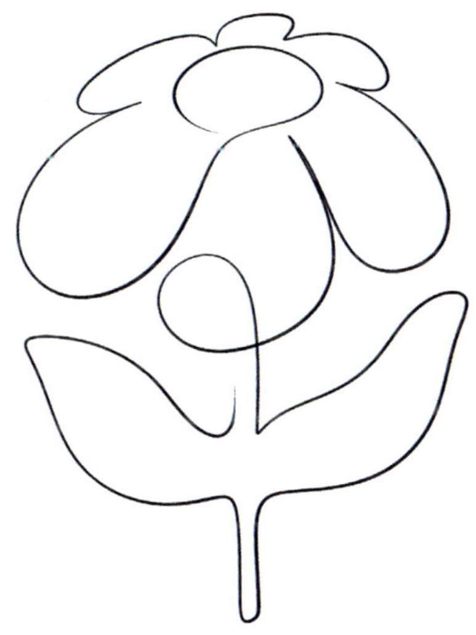

MINIMALISTIC ART

Minimalistic art aims to portray the simplest form of its subject. The common characteristics of minimalist art are limited use of colour and use of simplistic shapes. To draw this flower in a minimalist style, I used only black and focused only on the linework. I have also experimented with using the 'single line' technique – this is where the illustration is drawn using one continuous line.

COMPOSITION

To create my mantra, I used Photoshop, following the steps on pages 16–23 to prepare for my project. The practical media alternative for this artwork would be to use a media that gives a strong colour application, like acrylic paint or markers.

BACKGROUND

As the artwork in this piece is quite busy, I have used a minimal colour palette so that the background does not distract too much from the foreground. I set my canvas to light blue using the steps on pages 16–17, and then got to work on the illustrative elements of the background on new layers.

I drew the linework of the sky, grass, winding river and sun first, to define my sections. The linework needed to be bold enough to ensure all of the aspects of the artwork stood out and were clearly visible.

I then added colour to these elements on new layers below the outlines. I used the same light blue background colour for the sky and river. I drew the sun at a large scale using a bright yellow so it was clear to see behind the flower. As the sun is the furthest in the distance, I chose not to outline it as I had done with the other elements so that it became more of the background.

To create this background using a practical media alternative, you could apply paint for the blue background, and then, once this has dried, sketch out your illustrative background elements in pencil so that the different elements are clear for you to see. You can then add colour to your sections before going over your linework with a thicker liner to make them more defined as in the example artwork.

ELEMENTS

The flower is the main focus of this illustration, so I wanted to place it centrally on the page so that it took up the most space out of all the different elements. As with the process of drawing the background, I drew the linework for the flower first and then used a new layer below this to add the colour.

Behind the flower, I drew the main cloud line along the bottom of the page to show that the flower is growing above it, and I also added two smaller clouds in the distance to add some perspective to the artwork. Similarly to the flower, I first drew the linework for these clouds digitally before adding in the colour in a layer underneath. I also added some shadows on a new layer to the clouds to add some depth.

If you are working on your illustrative elements using practical media, you will need to be mindful about the order in which you are drawing your elements. Once you have your background elements in place (the sky, grass, winding river and sun), draw your clouds first, and then the main flower.

As this piece was inspired by retro design styles, I used a retro-inspired font called 'Gelica' to fit in with the artwork.

If you are drawing this mantra artwork by hand, I recommend looking at some retro-style lettering for inspiration and using this as a guide for your hand lettering. As the font in the example artwork is quite rounded, I would also recommend using a round-tip marker for your hand lettering.

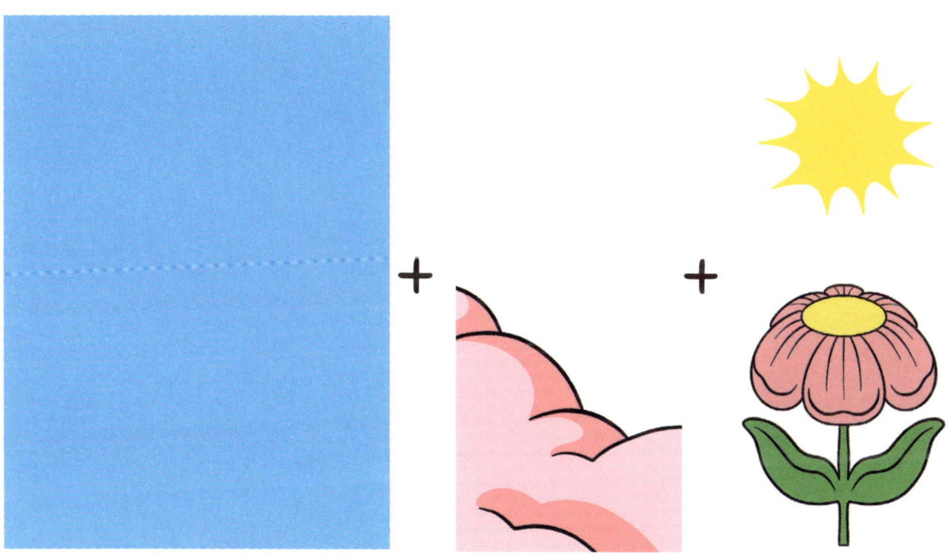

+ Keep Your Head Up

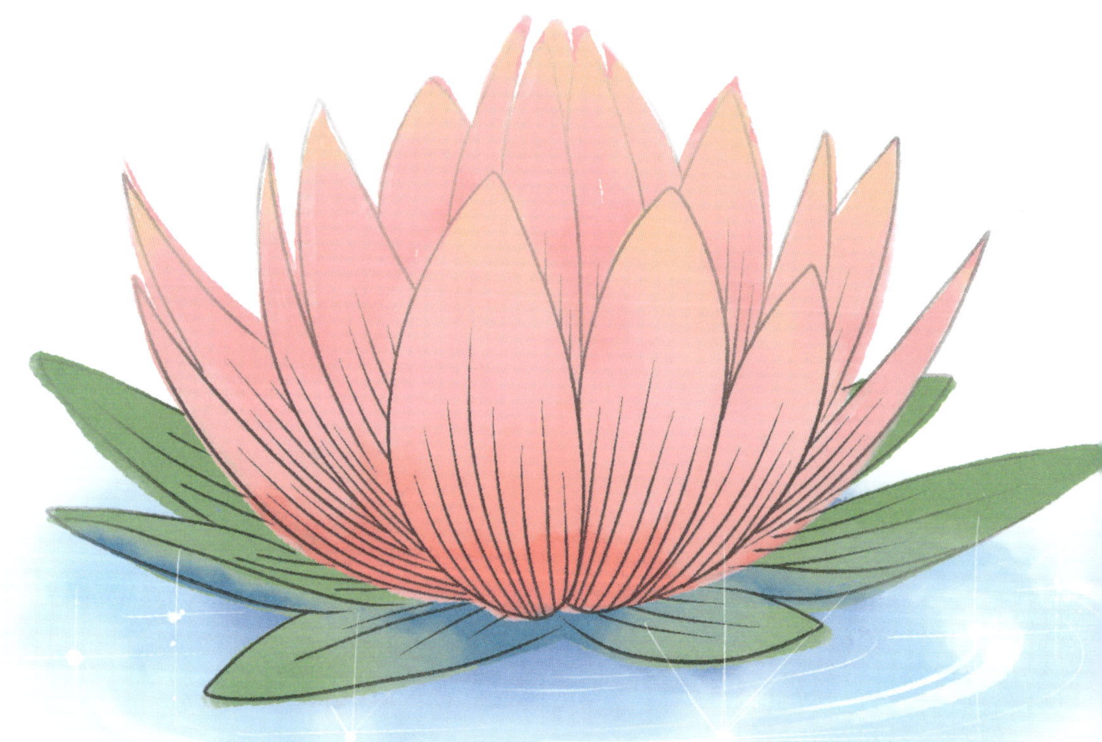
be kind to yourself

BE KIND TO YOURSELF

For many people, the idea of being kind to ourselves is not something that we are familiar with or that comes particularly easily. There are many ways we can show kindness to ourselves, as this is unique to each individual and depends on what brings us joy in our lives. Things such as allowing yourself time for your hobbies and interests may seem more straightforward. However, the idea of speaking to yourself more kindly may take more practice.

Being more mindful of how you speak to yourself, and making an effort to use more compassionate language, can have positive effects on your wellbeing by helping to reduce stress and allowing you to better cope with challenging situations.

In this chapter, we are going to use a relaxed watercolour technique to create the scene of a lotus flower floating on water under a full moon. By combining the soothing process of painting with watercolour with this calming mantra message, I hope to create a moment of calm for you while you create your artwork.

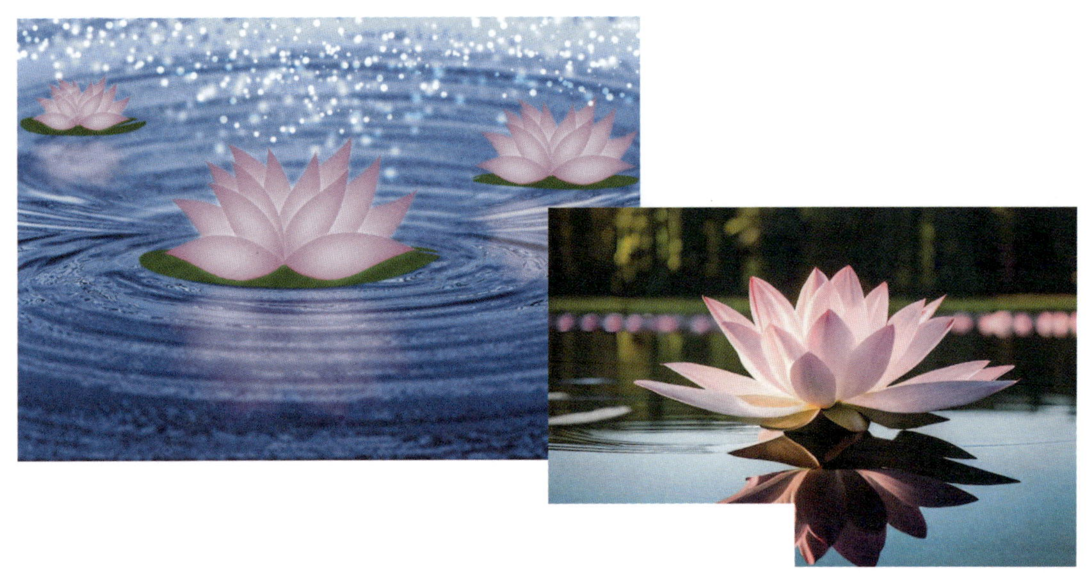

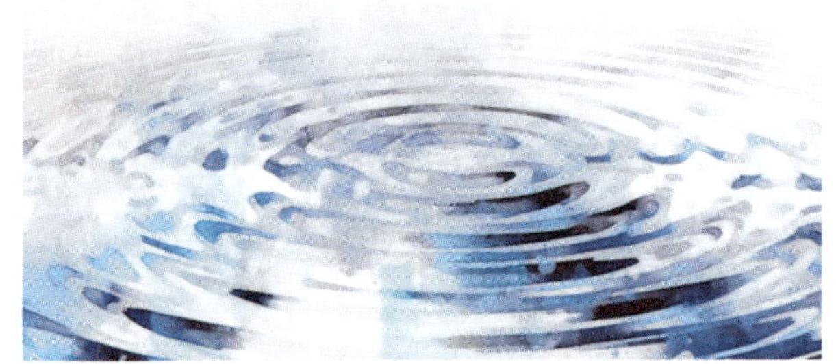

*watercolour
lotus in
rippled water*

be kind

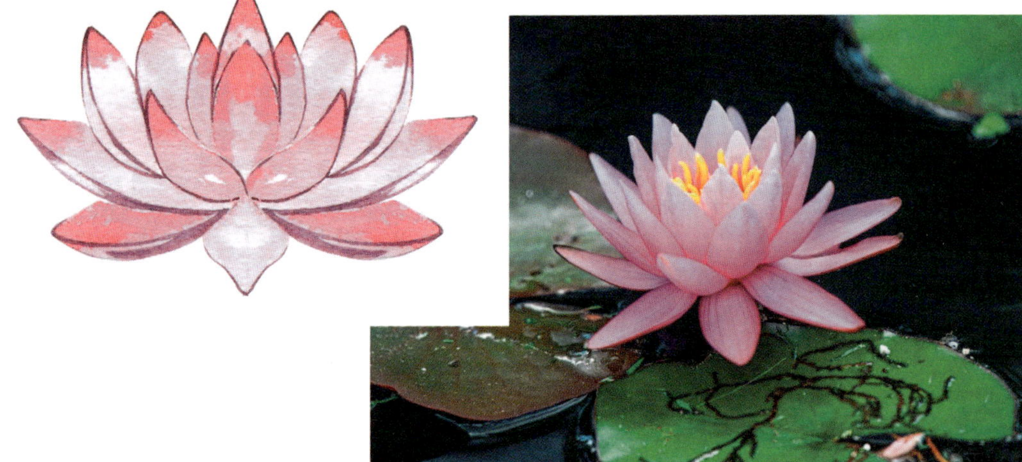

MANTRA MOOD BOARD

The purpose of this mantra artwork is to calm the viewer, so the inspiration for this illustration is a calm lotus flower sitting on top of the water in the light of the full moon. Lotus flowers in art are seen as a symbol for beauty and honesty rising from a dark place, so they are a great motif to illustrate being kind to yourself. The full moon is a symbol for transformation, which is a fitting metaphor for the positive transformation that being kind to yourself can shape.

I chose to use pink as the main colour in this artwork, as pink is the colour of love and compassion, and also a recognizable colour for the lotus flower. I have used realistic colours for the other aspects of the artwork: green for the leaves and blue for the water that the flower is floating on.

I want the lotus and moon in this illustration to have a bit more detail than in previous projects, to give us an opportunity to experiment with different styles of drawing and painting.

Experimenting with different styles is a very necessary process on your journey to figuring out your own personal style.

I want to add some rippling water to add some shadow underneath the lotus flower, and sparkles to add a mystical quality to it. The colour will need to be most dense directly underneath the lotus flower to show the shadow, and become lighter as it spreads out towards the edges of the page.

I'm going to use a brush pen for the lettering here to complement the watercolour-painted elements of the illustration. Calligraphic lettering creates a more fluid feel, which ties in with the aesthetic of this artwork.

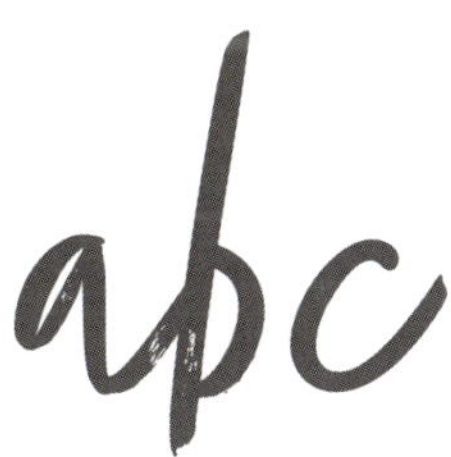

ADDING TEXTURE AND OVERLAYS

When adding colour to any illustration, I always start with blocking out the base colours of the objects. When drawing digitally, I usually utilize layers above my base colour layer with a clipping mask on to add additional texture and overlays if I want to add more depth to the artwork.

A clipping mask is a tool in Photoshop that allows you to draw on top of whatever is on the layer underneath. It's useful when adding detail to your drawings as you can colour freely on the page without going outside the lines of the shape on the layer beneath.

ADDING TEXTURE AND OVERLAYS DIGITALLY

Set up your canvas on Photoshop using the steps on pages 16–17. Here, we will go through the steps of drawing the lotus flower, from blocking out the colour to adding the final details using a clipping mask. For this activity, you may like to use a brush pen for steps 1 and 5, and a watercolour brush for steps 3–4.

1. Using the steps on pages 126–127, colour block out the very basic sections of your flower, adding each colour to a different layer. For my lotus flower, you can see that there is no definition in the petals or leaves, and the drawing looks two-dimensional. Once you are happy with your colours, move to the next step.

2. Create a new layer above the first layer of your colour-blocked lotus flower. Right click on the new layer and select 'Clipping mask'. This layer is where you will be adding your shadows, and you will need to create a new layer to sit on top of each part of your colour-blocked flower. In this scenario, there are three colour-blocked layers, so you will need to create three new layers, applying the 'Clipping mask' to each, and dragging each new layer to sit on top of the colour-blocked layer.

3. Once your layers are set up, draw shadows at the base of the petals and at the base of the leaves underneath the flower. The clipping mask will ensure your marks stay within the lines of your colour-blocked lotus. To create my shadows, I chose a colour slightly darker than the base colour, and added the shadows with quick brushstrokes, working up from the bottom of the petals. This is so they naturally fade out where the brush leaves the page and create a transition between the shadow colour and base colour.

4. Next, on the same layers, add highlights
    to the tips of the petals and leaves.
    I chose a colour that was slightly lighter
    than the base colour, using the same
    technique as the shadows.

5. Finally, to add more line detail to your
    flower, create a new layer to sit on top
    of all the other layers, and use light
    strokes with a brush pen to add in the
    outlines and detail lines in the petals
    and leaves. Don't worry too much about
    the colour being outside of lines, as this
    is in keeping with the style of the piece.

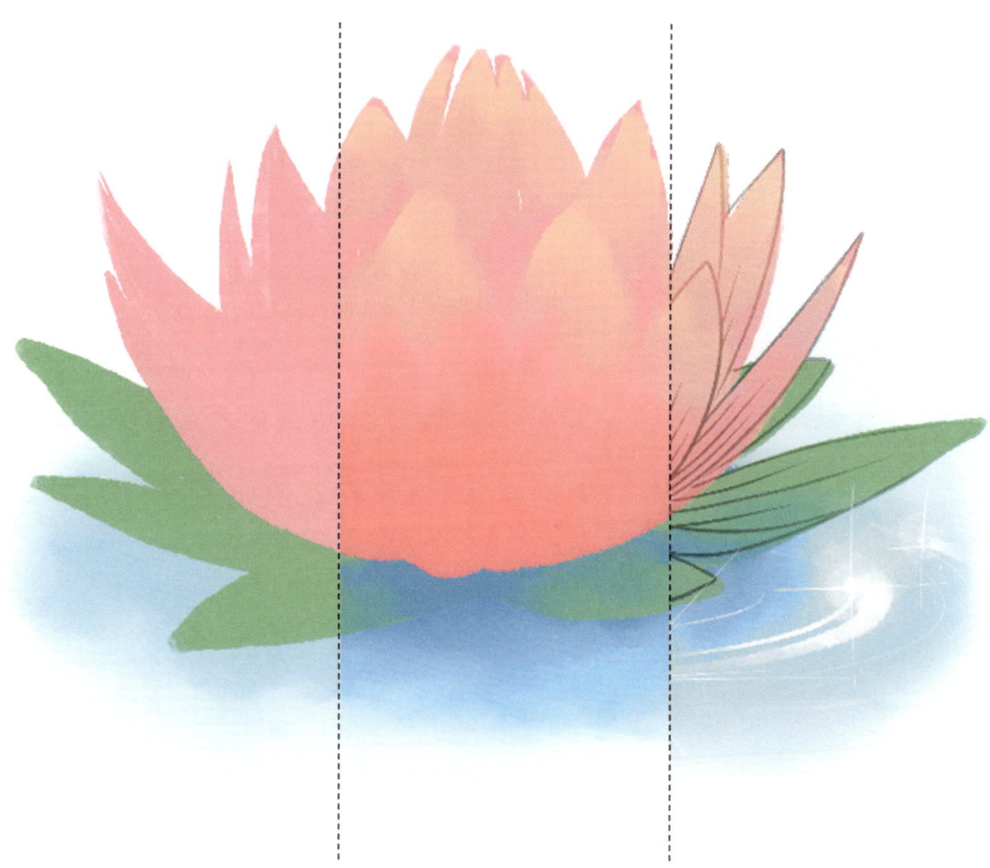

ADDING TEXTURE AND OVERLAYS PRACTICALLY

For this particular artwork, I would recommend using watercolour paint, as it is a great medium to use if you are looking to build texture up on a piece. We have previously discussed the importance of working in gradual layers with watercolour on pages 60–61, so make sure you are leaving enough time for your paint to dry between adding layers for this project.

1. When adding light and shade to a piece with watercolour, it's important to work from lightest to darkest. For the lotus in this project, you will want to work on the lightest, highlighted portions of the flower first. To begin, select a pink shade, and add more water to the paint to lighten the colour to your desired shade for your highlights. Start with your lightest layer of paint to fill in your lotus shape, leaving time for each layer to dry.

2. To gradually build up darker layers to define more shadows and details, simply add more paint pigment to your paint-to-water ratio to make your pink paint darker. You will want to apply the darker shade, working from the bottom of the petal upwards, using your brushstrokes to add the darker shades and working towards the base of the flower.

3. Once the paint has dried on your flower, follow the same process to add in the leaves by starting with the lightest green colour, and working towards to darker shades at the base of the leaves underneath the flower.

4. When you are happy with your flower and the paint has dried, you can use a thin brush pen or thin watercolour brush to add your outline and detail lines on the petals and leaves using light strokes. You don't want your outline to be too strong, so if you are using paint, I would recommend using a light mixture of black paint with a lot of water so it won't stand out too much from the other colours.

COMPOSITION

To create my mantra, I used Photoshop, following the steps on pages 16–23 to prepare for my project. For a practical media alternative for this artwork, using watercolour paint for the colour and a brush liner for the detail and mantra message will create the same effect, as you can see in the example illustration.

BACKGROUND

I began this mantra illustration by blocking out the colours of the lotus and water, using the steps on pages 60–61. Once the base colours were done, I added some detail with shadows and highlights, before adding the moon. I then added some fine details to the flower using light strokes towards the tips of the lotus leaves. Finally, I added some sparkles to the water.

I have included the steps to creating the elements for this piece practically on page 61.

TEXT

I added our mantra message in front of the moon using the 'Adlery Pro' font. When figuring out the sizing of the font, I decided to make it the same width as the flower in order to balance the composition.

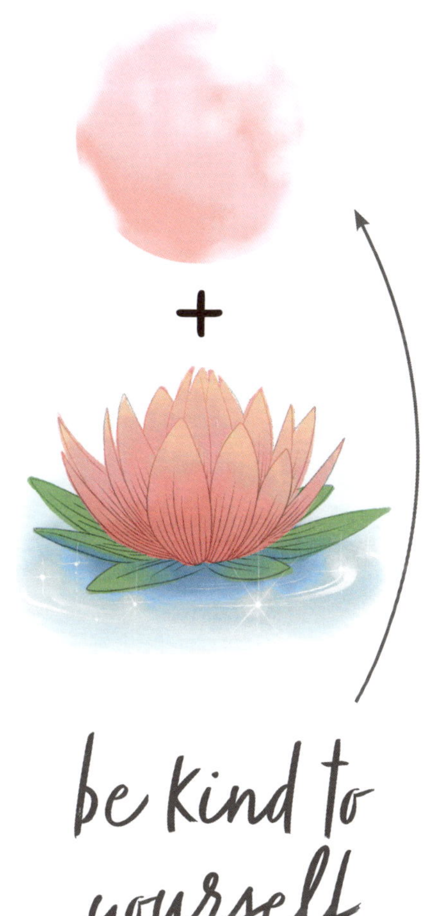

this too
shall
pass

THIS TOO
SHALL PASS

We all experience highs and lows throughout life, and the movement of the ocean seems a fitting metaphor for this. Watching the ocean from the shore, the water can seem calm one moment, but then a wave will form and crash down seemingly out of nowhere, before it disappears and the water seems calm once more.

This constant motion reflects the unpredictability of life. One moment, everything seems under control, and the next moment it feels as though a huge wave has come in and swept us off our feet. These moments can feel as overwhelming as if we're under water, but if you are able to give yourself the mental space to clear your head, you may find you are able to take steps to deal with whatever situation you are in and remember that this too shall pass.

In this chapter, we are using the abstracted image of a large wave as a metaphor for this mantra, and we are using a loose watercolour technique to try and capture the unpredictable motion of the water and remind us of its temporary nature.

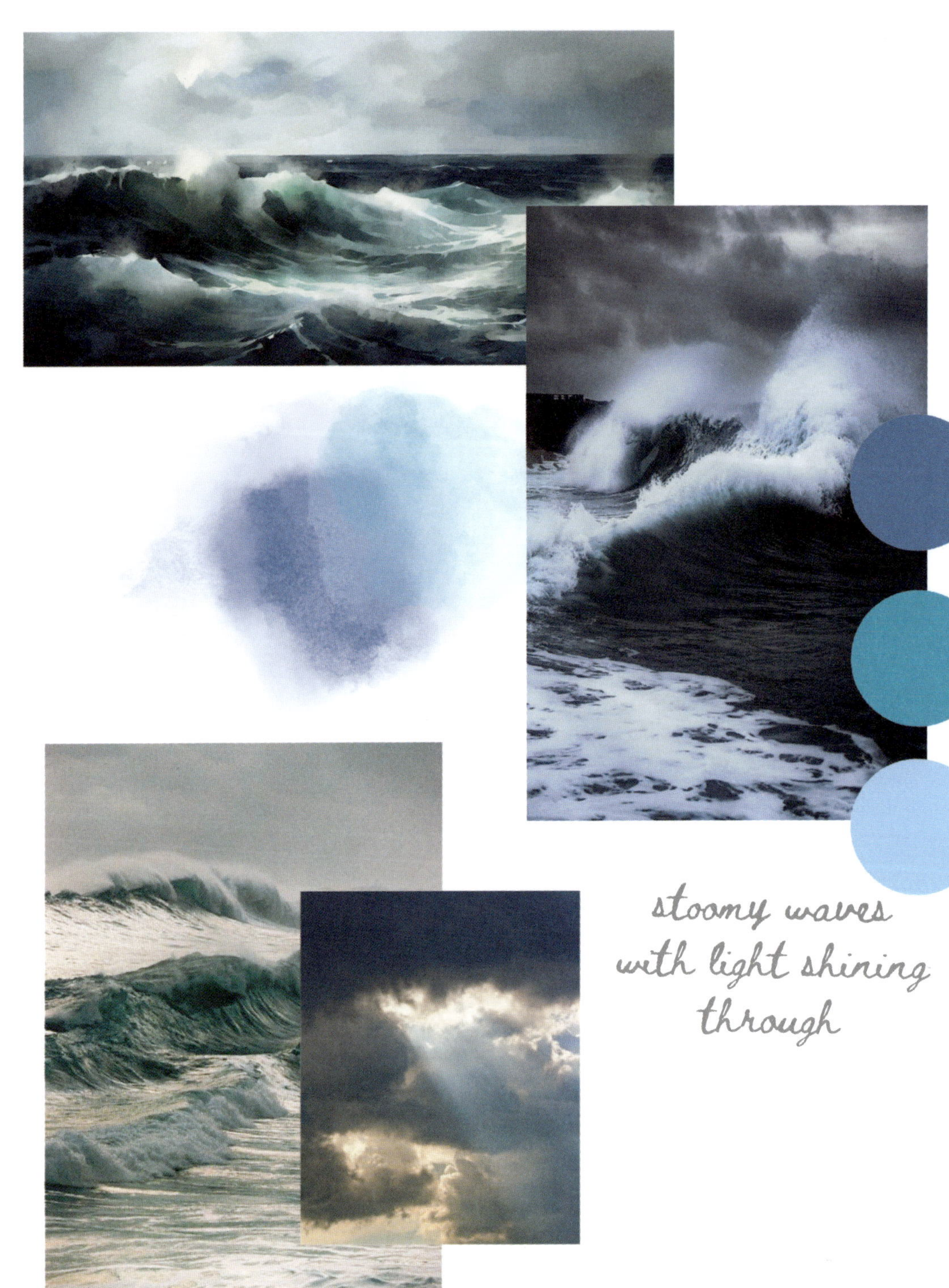
stormy waves
with light shining
through

MANTRA MOOD BOARD

The composition for this piece is very simple, and we'll be using the metaphor of a storm passing over the ocean to illustrate this mantra. Ocean waves are in a constant state of change and are a great symbol for transformation, so a large wave with some sunlight shining through it is going to form the background of this artwork.

I want to create the feeling of a wave washing over us with this piece, so I will use a realistic ocean colour palette here of different shades of blue.

The wave is going to be the background element of this artwork, so I'll be using loose watercolour brushstrokes to convey the motion of the water. I'll also add a few sparkles on the surface of the water to show the sunlight reflecting, and give the artwork a magical quality.

The mantra message is going to sit in front of the wave, so I'll be using a thick brush pen to make sure the message is clear against the background.

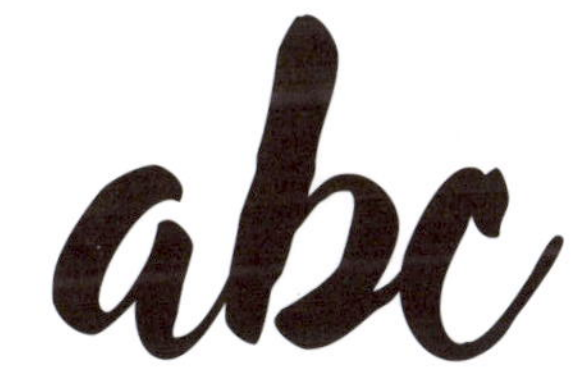

USING CALLIGRAPHY

Learning to write in calligraphy-style lettering is a very useful technique that you can use endlessly in your artwork to create text that is as eye-catching as it is beautiful. To understand calligraphy, you need to understand the 'thick and thin' style that comes from using a calligraphy nib rather than a regular pen, which has a rounded nib. Calligraphy nibs are broad and flat, and manipulating this to create different thicknesses of lines gives you this 'thick and thin' style.

To work with calligraphy digitally using software like Photoshop, you will need to set up your canvas (see pages 16–17) and find a calligraphy brush. If you are using Photoshop, you can find a set of calligraphy brushes within the 'Legacy Brushes' set (see page 60). If you cannot find a suitable calligraphy brush, you may need to purchase and install a set of calligraphy brushes. For help installing brushes, there are many resources online that will be able to walk you through the stages based on your chosen software.

To write in a calligraphic style practically, you will need a piece of paper, ink and a calligraphy pen. Follow the steps opposite when using either the digital or practical approach.

WRITING USING CALLIGRAPHY

The fundamental rules of calligraphy are to create thick strokes when moving the pen up or down, and thin strokes when moving the pen side to side.

For example, if you look at the lettering we are using in this mantra artwork, you will notice that the parts of the letters that are vertical have been written using thick strokes, and the parts that are horizontal are using the thin strokes. The whole effect creates lettering that appears fluid and smooth.

With calligraphy, you usually connect (or 'join up') each letter within your word, with the exception of any capital letters at the start of a word. Once you have mastered the basic skills of using thick and thin strokes and connecting your letter, you may wish to move on to more complicated forms of calligraphy, which focus on adding further embellishments and flair to the letters.

TOP TIPS

A couple of tips to follow when writing with a calligraphy nib are:

Keep the nib at a constant angle as you are writing (this means not rotating your hand or paper as you follow the curves of your letters).

Use light pressure when writing. Lead the pen and don't push against the paper. This creates an even flow of ink between the letters.

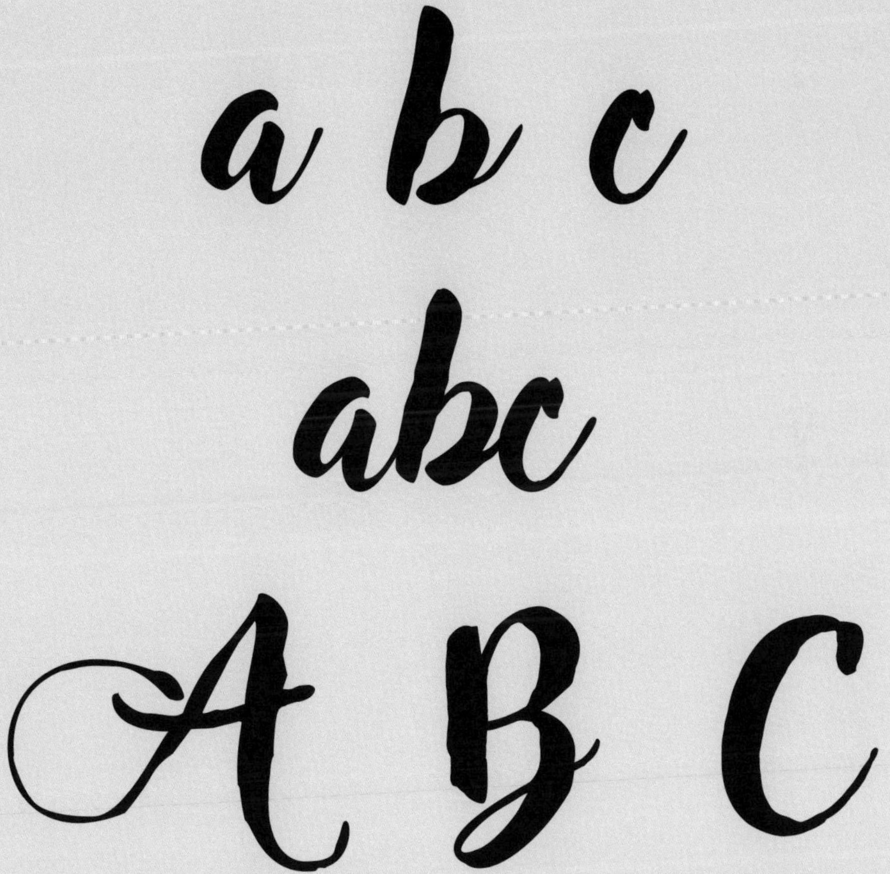

COMPOSITION

To create my mantra, I used Photoshop, following the steps on pages 16–23 to prepare for my project. The practical media alternative is traditional watercolour, a thick ink pen for the calligraphy section and a white marker for the sparkles. If using watercolour, be sure all of the water has dried between each layer before you start writing.

ELEMENTS

I began painting my wave background by adding in the base colours and blocking out the shape of the wave. I didn't worry about creating a really defined shape at first, as I knew I would add more definition throughout the process.

I then added in some shadows in a darker blue to create some depth to the wave at the top and bottom of the curve. Next, I added some definition to the wave shape with a thinner brush. I then added some final splashes to add the motion of the wave, and finally, I incorporated a few sparkles here to show the light reflecting on the water.

TEXT

I added my lettering on top of my elements. I used the font 'Adlery Pro', but you can also use the instructions on pages 118–119 to add your own hand lettering in either Photoshop or pen. I played around with the size and placement until I was happy with it, experimenting with smaller and larger text until I found the size that felt most at home at the centre of the wave.

To add your own hand lettering using a practical medium, you can use a thick pen or calligraphy pen, following the steps on page 119. You may like to sketch out your writing in pencil first to use as a guideline.

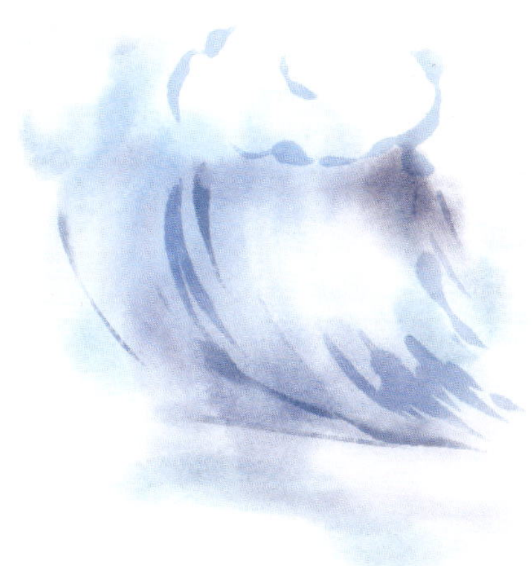

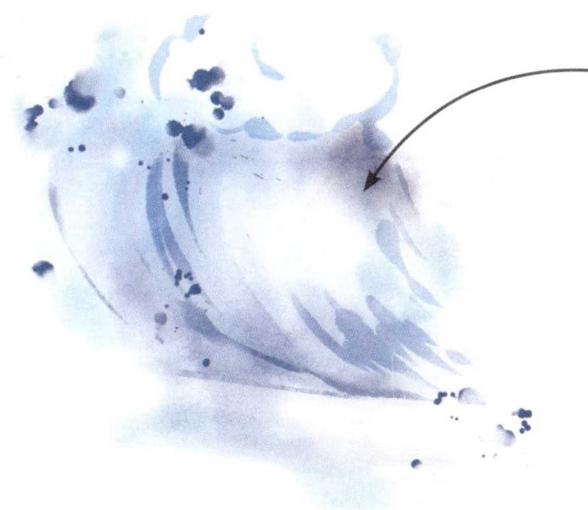

this too
shall
pass

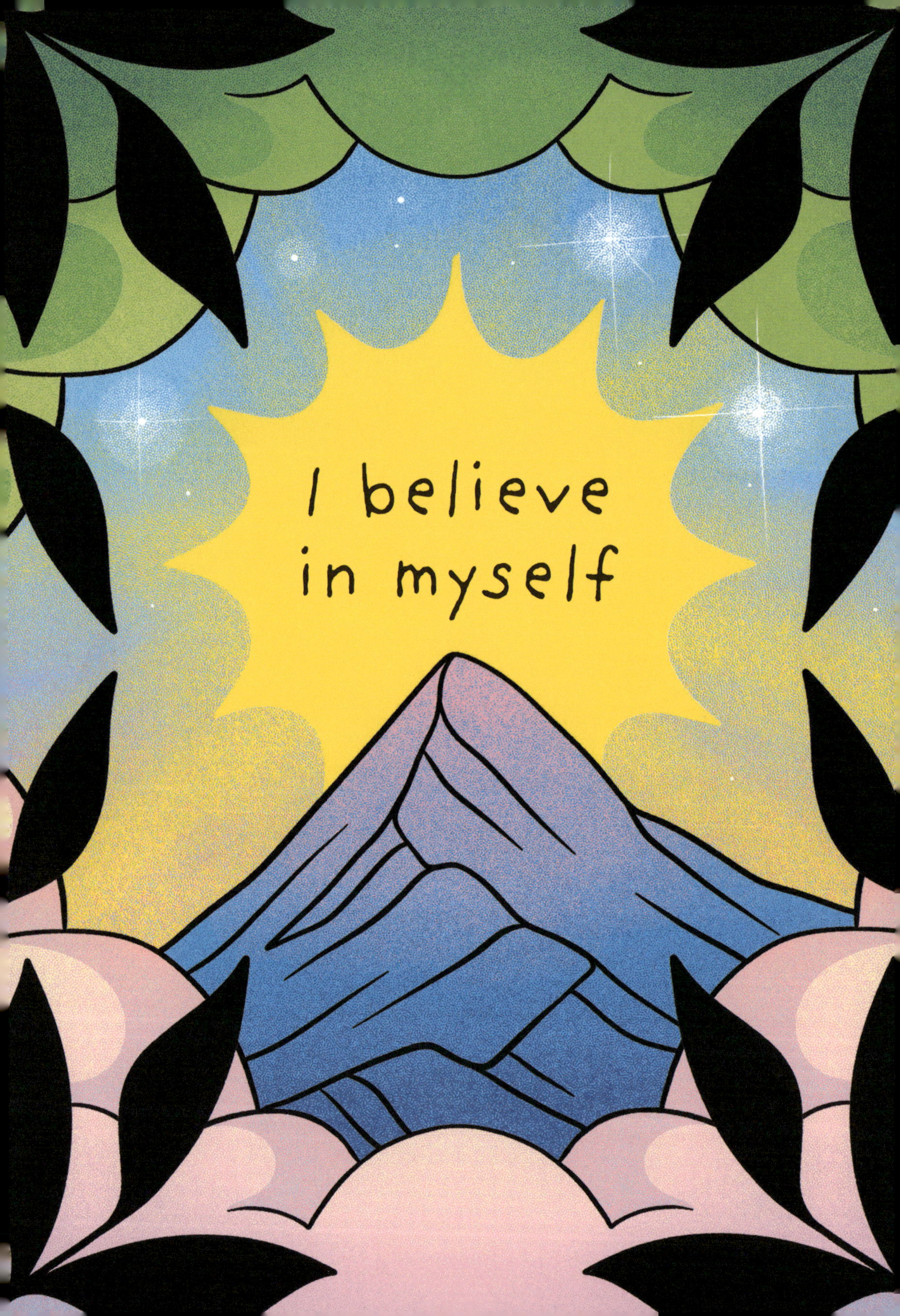

I believe
in myself

I BELIEVE IN MYSELF

What does it mean to believe in yourself? Your self-belief is shaped from many things including your sense of self-worth, your self-confidence and the amount of trust you have in yourself and your abilities. Believing in yourself is the foundation that will allow you to overcome self-doubt and work towards achieving your goals.

The journey to believing in yourself may not be a straightforward one, as learning to deconstruct your self-doubts and work towards building positive self-talk can take time and effort. But it will have continual benefits that will help you get to where you want to be.

In this chapter we are going to use the image of a mountain peak as a metaphor for this mantra, to symbolize the journey to believing in yourself. As this mantra artwork is intended to inspire, we are going to use a fantasy-inspired style and colour palette to create an artwork that will embolden you to achieve your dreams!

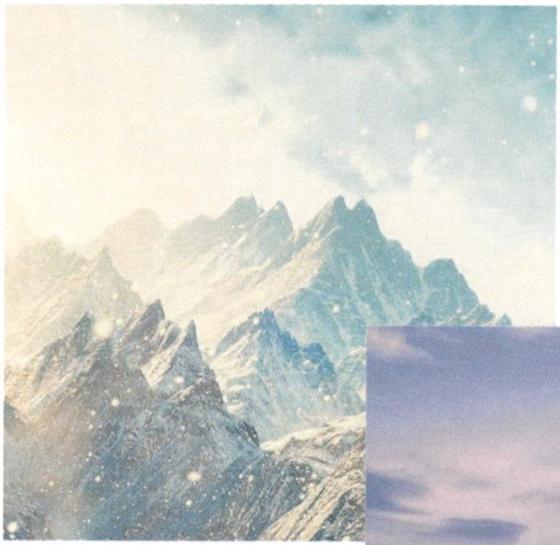

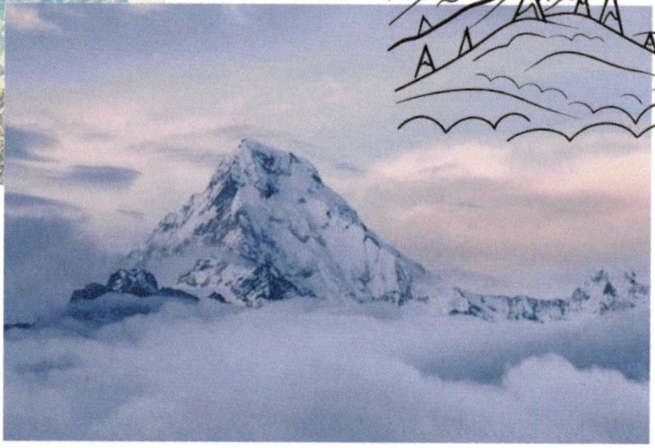

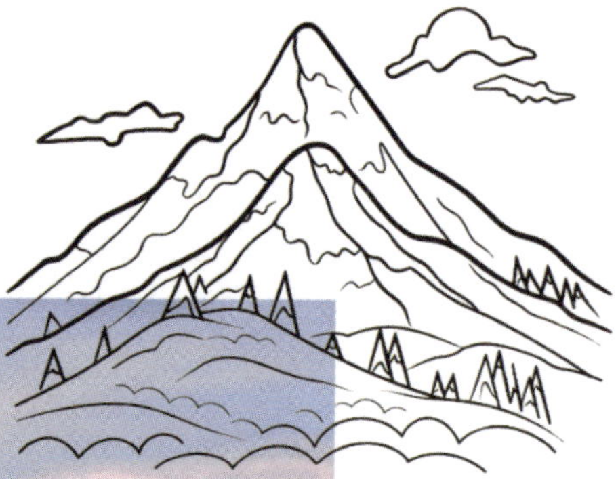

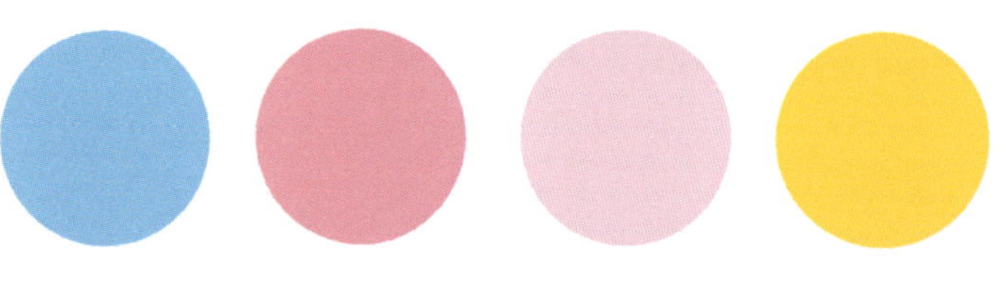

mountain
above clouds
through
forest

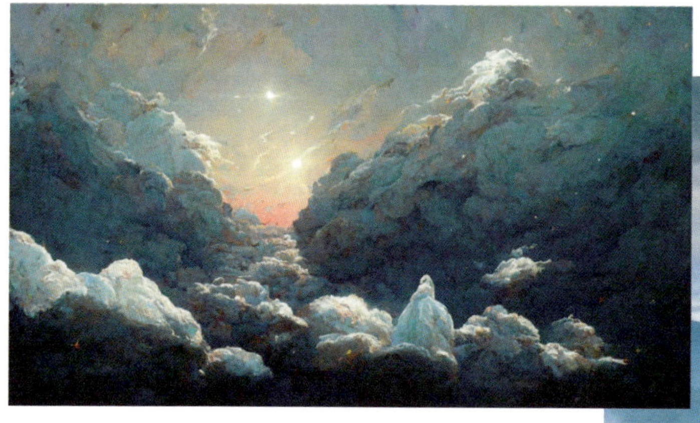

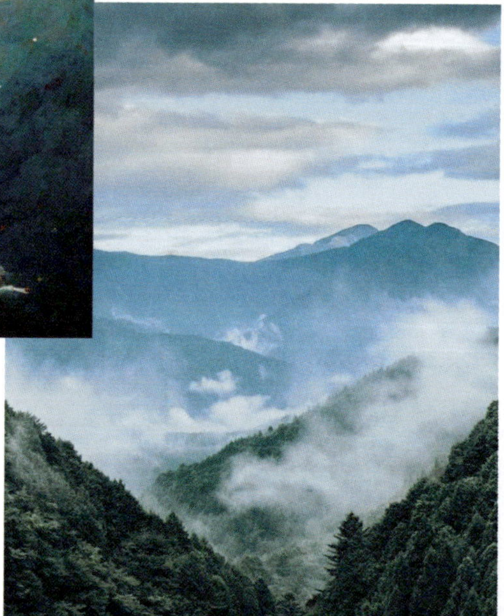

I believe

MANTRA MOOD BOARD

The topic for this artwork is a mountain peak rising above the clouds through a leafy woodland frame and, as we want this to be a motivational mantra, we are going to use a bold illustration style with bright colours. There are a lot of layers of colour in this artwork, so I'll be teaching you how to use colour blocking to help decide on the colour scheme and layout for your piece before you create your final piece.

I want to work with a more fantasy-inspired colour palette in this piece, with exaggerated colours for each of the motifs featured in this illustration. This piece should be inspiring and motivating, so I hope that the highly saturated colours used here will help to achieve that.

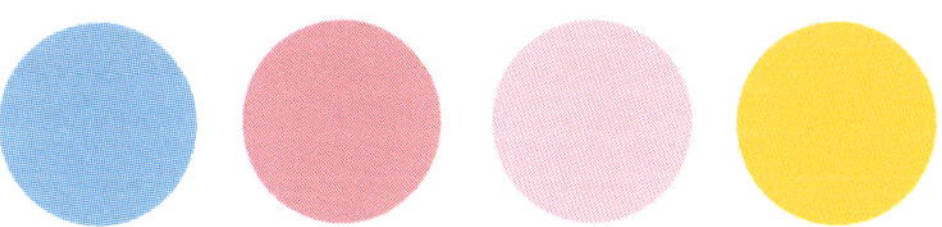

The sun will be large in the centre of the illustration as a symbol for positivity and hope. I'll be drawing the sun without an outline, as the mantra message is going in front of it, and I don't want any lines crossing over and obscuring the lettering.

The mountain landscape will be framed with leaves and a tree canopy at the top, to give a frame to the artwork and direct the eye to the central message.

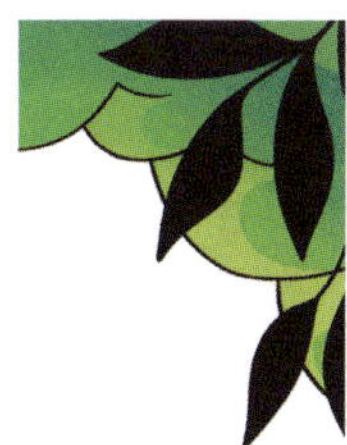

A large mountain in the centre of the artwork will symbolize a challenge to be overcome, and give the artwork a sense of height. The clouds around the mountain base will illustrate how high the peak is by showing it as above the cloud line.

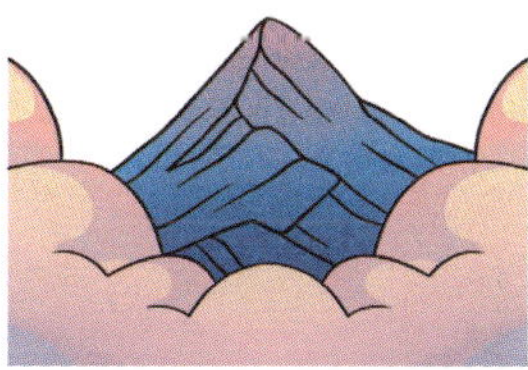

Our mantra message will be written inside the sun so it is clear to read in the landscape.

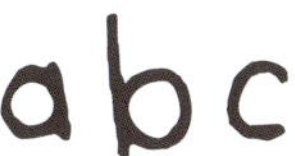

COLOUR BLOCKING

This is a useful technique for working out your composition and the colour palette you would like to use. It is helpful to get your base colours down at the same time so you can see how they work together and whether you need to make any changes before you start working on the detail. It's much easier to do this in the early stages than later down the line!

A common edit I have to make in my illustrations is changing the colour of the sky to make the sun look bright enough. If you colour block first, you can edit the colour of the sky effortlessly. You can see the difference from the first image with the original sky blue that I chose, and the final version that is used in the mantra artwork.

COLOUR BLOCKING USING PHOTOSHOP

1. To begin, set up your canvas in Photoshop using the steps on pages 16–17.

2. Create your first layer using the steps on pages 18–19. This is where you will block out the first colour for your piece.

3. To block out your first colour, you can either draw your lines and colour them in using the 'Brush' tool (see page 20), or you can draw your lines with the 'Brush' tool and use the 'Paint bucket' tool in the left-hand toolbar to fill the shape in.

4. Repeat step 3 for each colour or element of your piece, creating a new layer for each part of the drawing. This way, you can easily adjust the colours separately.

5. If you need to change the colour of a layer once you have finished your colour blocking, simply use the 'Colour picker' tool to pick your new colour, and use the 'Paint bucket' tool to change the colour of your layer by clicking on the item on the layer.

COLOUR BLOCKING USING A PRACTICAL MEDIUM

You can colour block by hand using most practical medium; however, the method will be different for each medium. Colour blocking can be trickier for mediums such as pencil, watercolour or pastel, so for this exercise, I recommend using something like acrylic paint that produces a strong colour application.

It isn't as easy to change your colours using a practical medium once you have put them on the page, so I would recommend doing some colour swatches of your palette with the swatches next to each other so you can see how they work together before going onto your final canvas or page. Alternatively, you can take the opportunity to practise this on a separate piece of paper or canvas, with the intention of mimicking and recreating it for your final piece down the line.

1. Select your canvas or piece of paper, and gather your materials (for example, acrylic paint and paintbrushes).

2. Apply each layer of colour to your piece one at a time, allowing enough time for each layer to dry between applications. If you are using pastels or watercolours for your piece, you might prefer to sketch out an outline of your piece first using pencil, and then colour in the lines. This will prevent you from building up too many layers on your piece, and ensure you can see the colours properly without them mixing together.

3. If you are unhappy with a colour once the piece is complete, you may be able to loosely repaint over the layer. Or, you may need to begin again from scratch, and embrace the process of experimentation!

COMPOSITION

To create my mantra, I used Photoshop, following the steps on pages 16–23 to prepare for my project. There are a lot of layers of colour in this artwork, so the practical media alternative would be acrylic paint, which allows you to create the bold colours. You can use a marker or fine liner for the linework and lettering for our mantra message.

ELEMENTS

I began this illustration by blocking out the base colours of the landscape using the steps on pages 126–127. Once the colours and shapes were blocked out, I added some light and shadows to create some depth to the landscape. As the sun in this composition provides the light source, I made sure I put the lighter areas closest to it.

Next, I added some finer details using texture, and included some more light and shadows to define the shape of the clouds and trees, and some sparkling stars. Finally, I added in the linework and the leaf frame.

To create your background practically, use the steps on page 127 to colour block your piece first. I advise using acrylic paint for this project.

Once you have colour blocked your piece, you'll need to start working into your sections with highlights and shadows. If you need some guidance here, think about the parts of the landscape the sun would naturally hit to create the highlights, and the parts of the landscape that would be the most shaded.

For the finer details, use white paint or a white gel pen to add the stars and a watery mix of paint to create the translucent effect of the additional highlights and shadows on the clouds. For the black linework I would recommend using a fine-liner pen, and black acrylic paint for the leaves in the foreground of the artwork.

TEXT

This artwork is meant to evoke the kind of motivational images you would see as a child, so I wanted to use a more childlike lettering to further this feeling. I am using the font 'Providence Sans Pro' to create this effect digitally.

To add your own hand lettering using a practical medium, you can use a thick pen or calligraphy pen, following the steps on page 119. You may like to sketch out your writing in pencil first to use as a guideline.

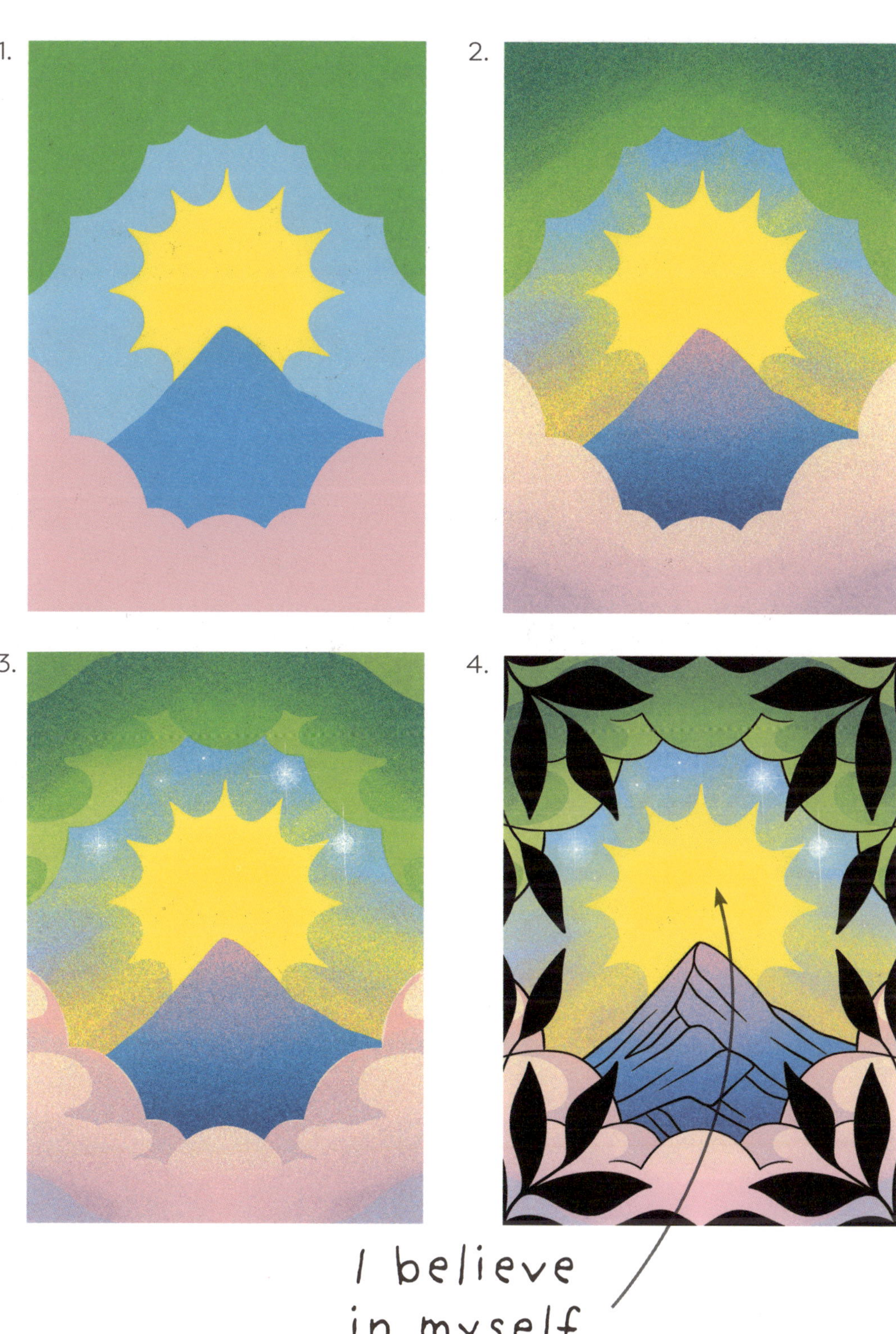
1.
2.
3.
4.
I believe
in myself

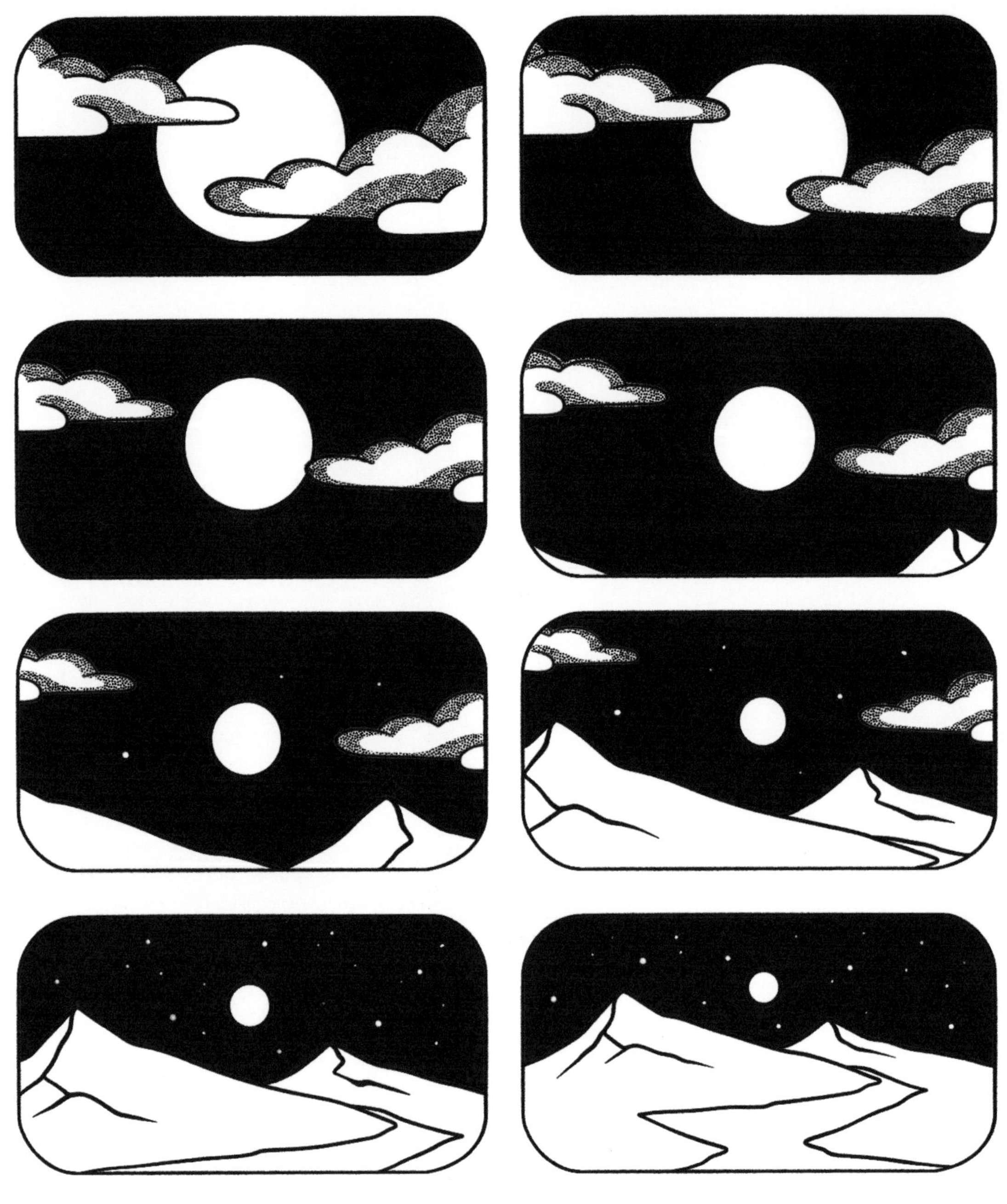

TAKE A STEP BACK

TAKE A
STEP BACK

Many of us have experienced times in our lives when things build up to the point where we feel overwhelmed, whether this is having a to-do list that's too much for us to complete, or a few bad days that make us feel like we'll never get through the week.

When we feel overwhelmed it can be difficult to think clearly and make sense of any situation or figure out where to start to take steps to work through it. But if we are able to take a physical or mental step back from whatever we're going through, it can give us some perspective that will allow us to figure out how we can move forward.

In this chapter, we are going to be using a grid layout to depict the motion of 'zooming out' on a landscape to reveal the full image as a metaphor for taking a step back from a situation to make sense of the full picture. We are also going to be experimenting with using a single colour in our palette to create our artwork, as this is in-keeping with our mantra message of trying to simplify our obstacles in order to tackle them.

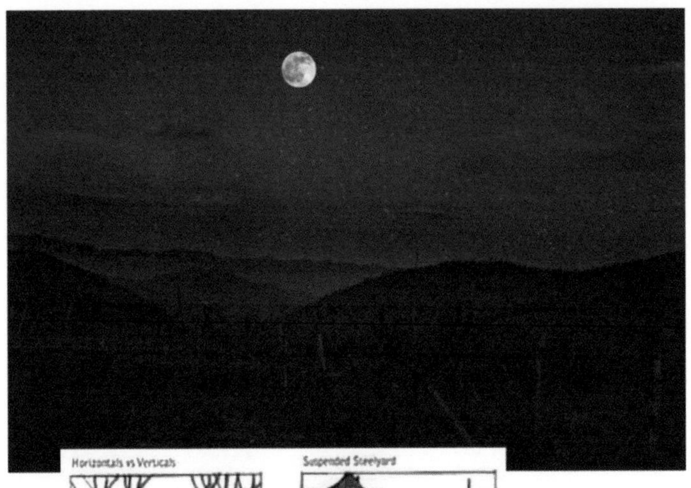

STEP
BACK

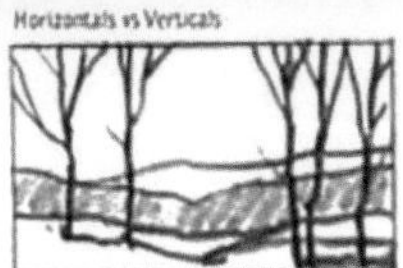

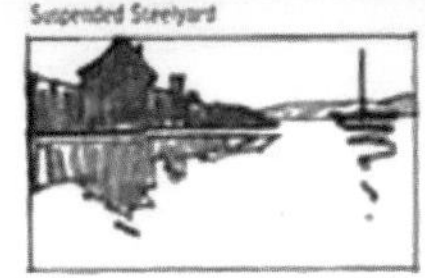

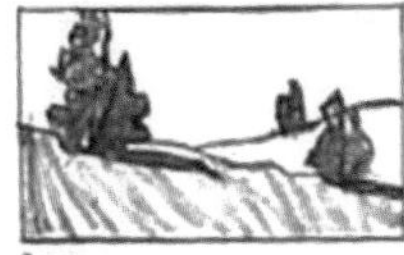

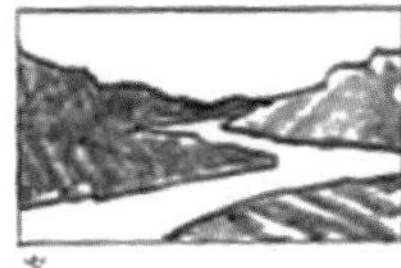

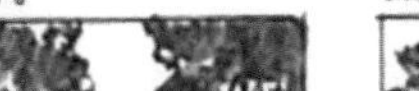

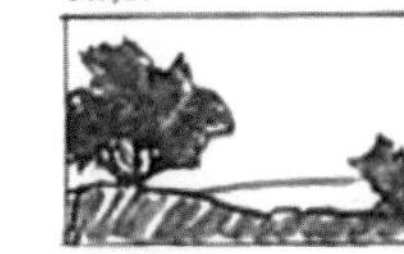

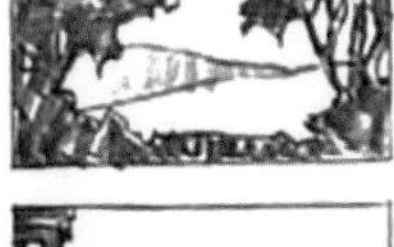

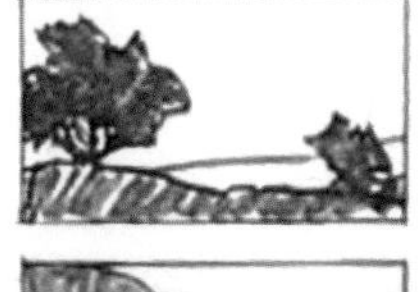

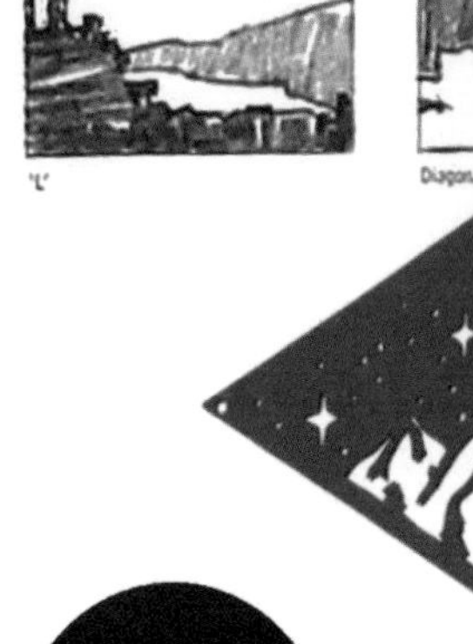

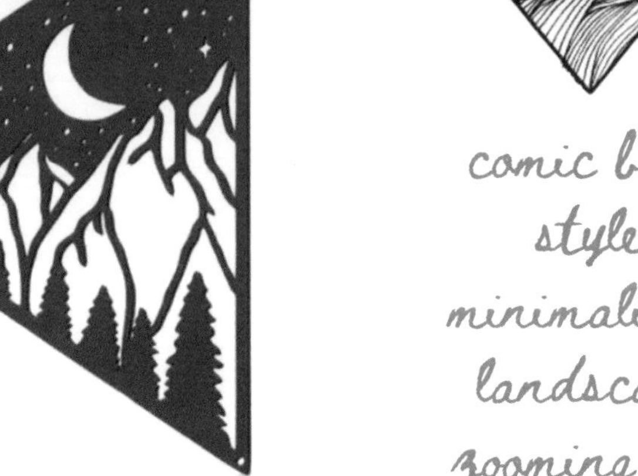

comic book
style
minimalistic
landscape
zooming out

MANTRA MOOD BOARD

Using the technique of storyboarding through grids (see pages 94–95), the inspiration for this artwork is to illustrate the idea of 'taking a step back' by zooming out on a landscape. We'll be using a comic book style layout for this artwork, so we can draw a different stage of zooming out in each frame, and we'll also be using just one colour to create a simpler, monochromatic piece that keeps the piece simple and calming.

The idea behind this mantra artwork is that by taking a step back, you may be able to simplify something that seems more complex, so I will use a single colour in this palette to help illustrate this idea of simplifying.

I'm also going to use simple motifs so that the artwork doesn't become too complex. The main features of each frame will be different views of the moon, clouds and mountains.

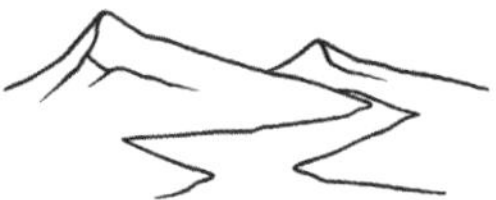

I'm going to use a bold, comic book-esque style of lettering to suit the bold, graphic style of the illustration.

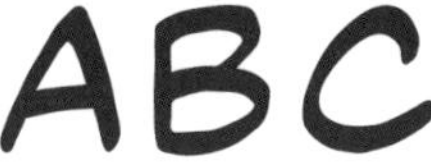

I want to draw multiple versions of the same landscape to tell a story to fit the mantra, so I'm going to use an eight-frame layout to guide me.

USING JUST ONE COLOUR

You may think that by using a single colour in your palette, you will have less to think about when creating your drawing. But using one colour will bring up other considerations that you will need to keep in mind during your process. Using our mantra artwork as an example, we will go through the decisions that I made while drawing this piece and how I came to them, and the different techniques you can use to add more detail to your artwork using just one colour. Whether you are using a practical medium or digital method to create your piece, the following theory will apply to help you develop your artwork.

Before you begin marking out your highlights and shadows, think about the shade of the colours as they would be in reality. In this mantra artwork, we are depicting a night-time scene, so the colour of the sky is black. In contrast to this, the moon and clouds are left white so they stand out against the background of the sky. The mountain and river landscape has also been left white as the mantra suggests that the more you step back from a situation, the more you will be able to see, so I wanted there to be a contrast in the zoomed-out frame of the landscape to illustrate this different view.

HOW TO DRAW USING ONE COLOUR

When drawing in one colour, it is easiest to start out with a basic sketch of your piece before figuring out which parts you want to be your highlights (the parts that you will leave white), your shadows (the parts that you will colour in), and the parts you would like shaded (if you are including any shading).

Top tip

If you are struggling to gauge which areas of your drawing should be light or dark, look at a black-and-white reference photo of the scene or elements you would like to draw. This will help you to see the light and dark areas more clearly, and help inform your choices.

ALTERNATIVE WAYS OF DRAWING USING ONE COLOUR

If you are still unsure whether an element of your artwork should be light or dark, you may like to experiment by playing around with different options for this element. For example, in this piece, the mountain could be either light or dark, depending on the reference image you are looking at or your personal style choice.

If you wanted to draw this piece with the mountains coloured black, something you would need to consider is how you would make them stand out against the sky. One way of doing this would be to draw your linework detail in white rather than black, as you can see in the first example here.

Another option to help further contrast your element if you are drawing two light or two dark objects next to one another is to add outlines to the different elements so that they contrast. In this second example, I have added a black outline to the cloud, which helps create a bit of space between the moon and the cloud, to separate and more clearly define these two light elements.

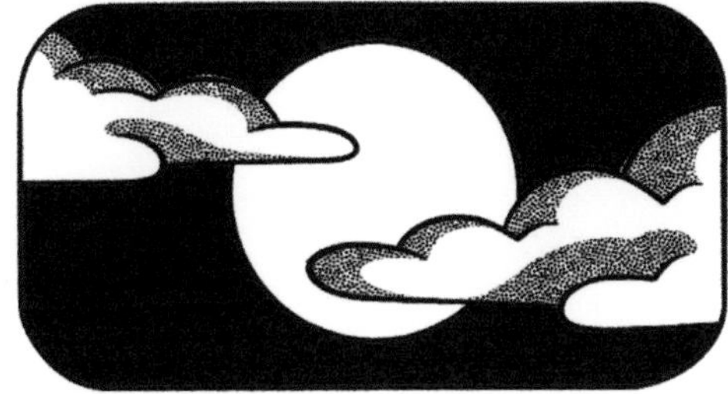

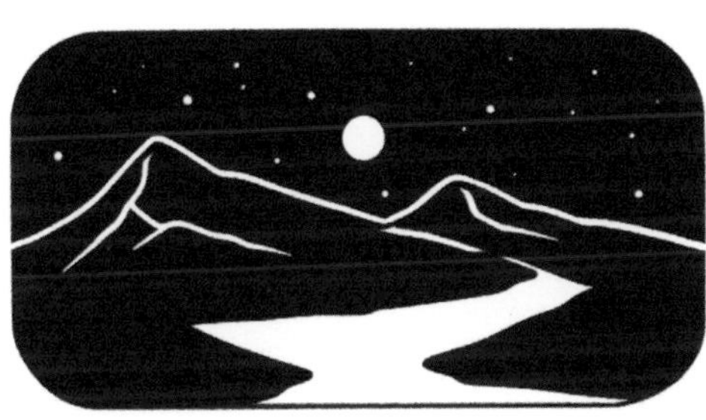

COMPOSITION

To create my mantra, I used Photoshop, following the steps on pages 16–23 to prepare for my project. The practical media alternative for this artwork would be fine-liner pens for your linework and detail, and a thicker marker pen to fill in your shadowed areas.

BACKGROUND

I began this artwork by drawing out a storyboard layout (see steps on pages 94–95), using eight rounded rectangles of the same size.

If you're using a practical method, sketch out your grid in pencil first using the method on page 95.

ELEMENTS

Next, I began to draw in the landscapes using the hard round brush. Each frame is a more zoomed-out view than the previous one, so I kept this changing scale in mind when drawing in the landscape elements. I then added in some details and depth to the artwork by including some shadows in the clouds, and some stars on the bottom four frames.

The practical media alternative for this piece would be fine-liner pens for the detail, and a black marker to fill in the dark space. The drawing process is the same practically as it is digitally. Start by drawing in the linework for all of the elements in the frames, then use your marker to fill in the areas that are shaded.

TEXT

Finally, using the font 'Intan', I added in our mantra message in the centre of the page underneath the illustration.

If you are writing your text by hand, using block capitals will work as a substitution for the style of the typed font.

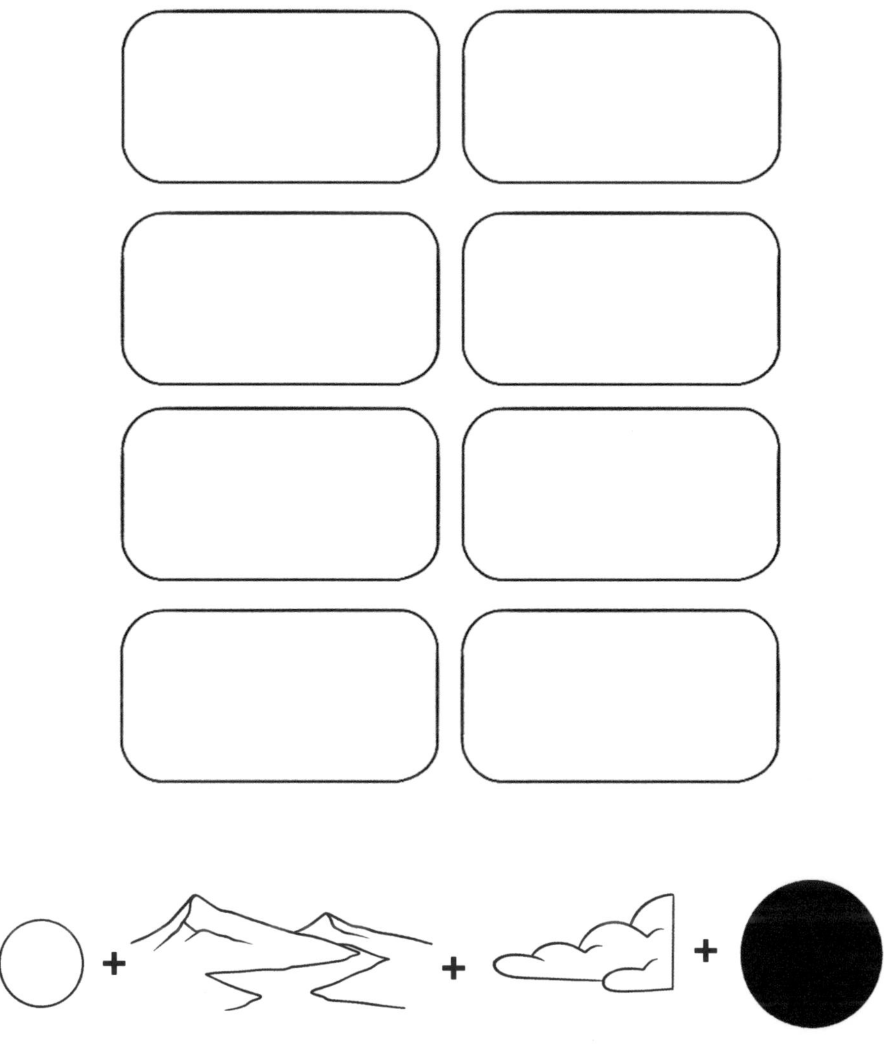

+ TAKE A STEP BACK

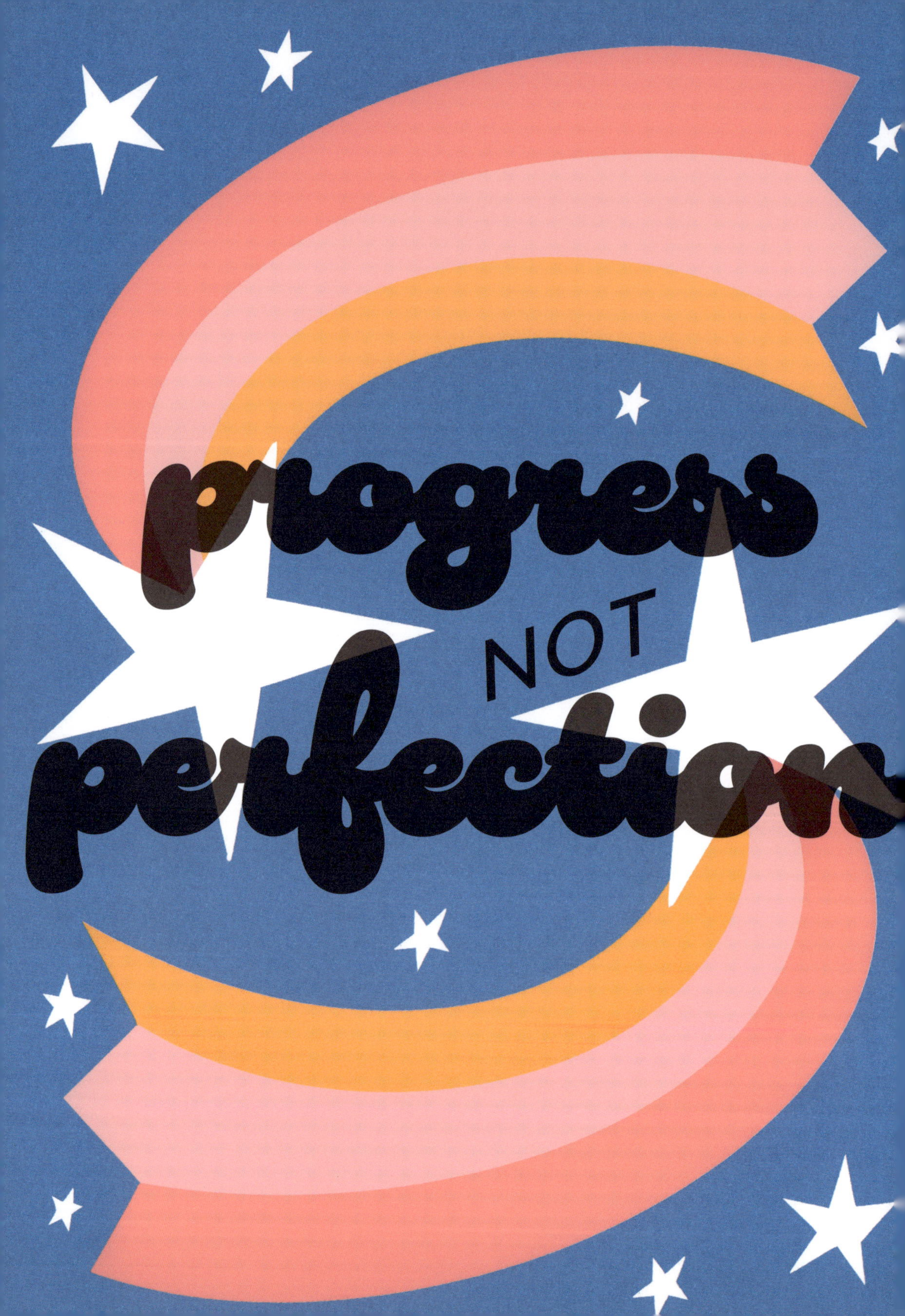

progress
NOT
perfection

PROGRESS
NOT PERFECTION

Perfectionism is defined by having high expectations and high standards for ourselves. This may sound like a great trait to have, but as we and our circumstances change over time, your idea of 'perfect' may change, and you could be forever making small tweaks to things and never feel like you get to the point where something is perfect.

The idea of progress over perfection encourages a shift from focusing on the perfect outcome to focusing on your growth and the things you have learned along the way. By placing more value on your growth, you will hopefully feel freer to experiment and learn from your experiences, whether you see them as good or bad.

In this project, we are going to look at how we can use the skills we have learnt so far so create two different mantra artworks to evoke different emotions from the viewer – one calming and one inspirational. We will discuss the aspects of the artwork that we will need to consider, and why certain artistic choices have been made.

This project is a great opportunity for you to experiment with different styles and see what emotions they evoke in you. Take notice of this, and use it to influence the choices you will make to produce your two artworks.

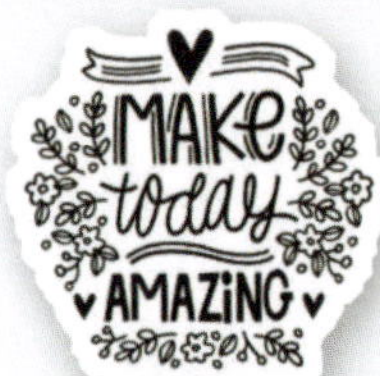

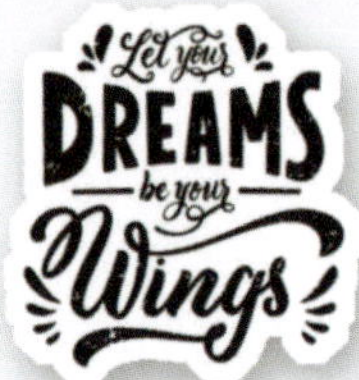

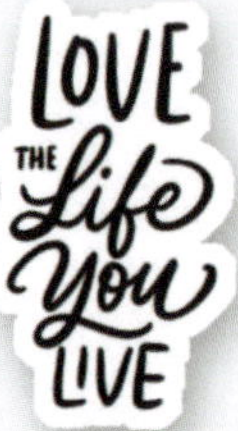

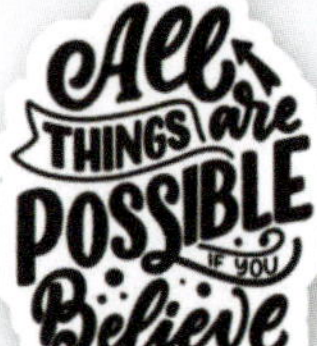

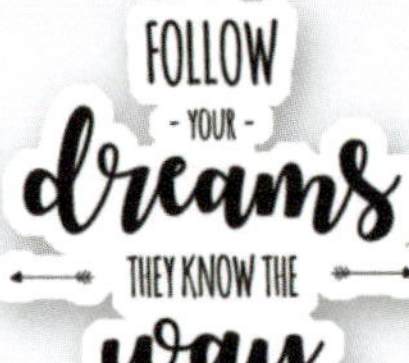

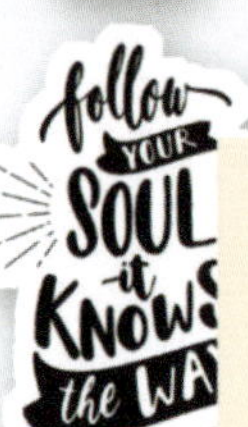

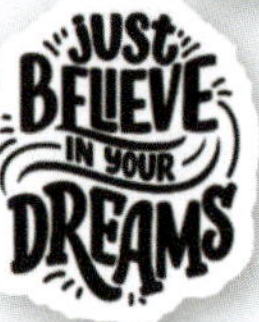

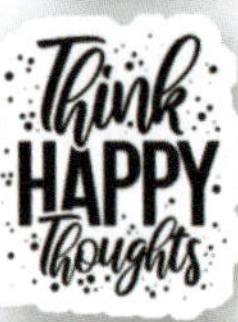

progress

Lettering
main focus

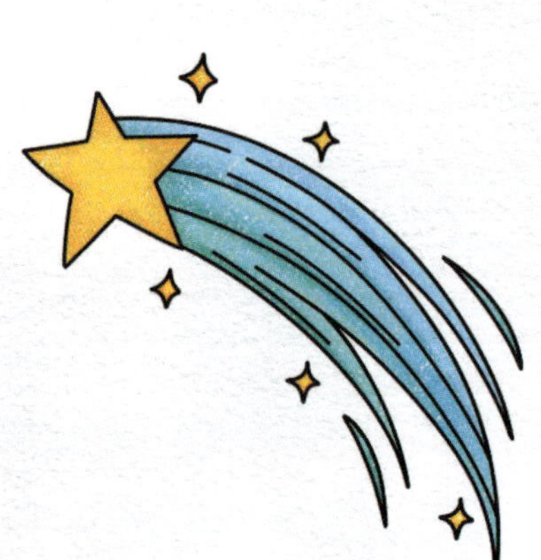

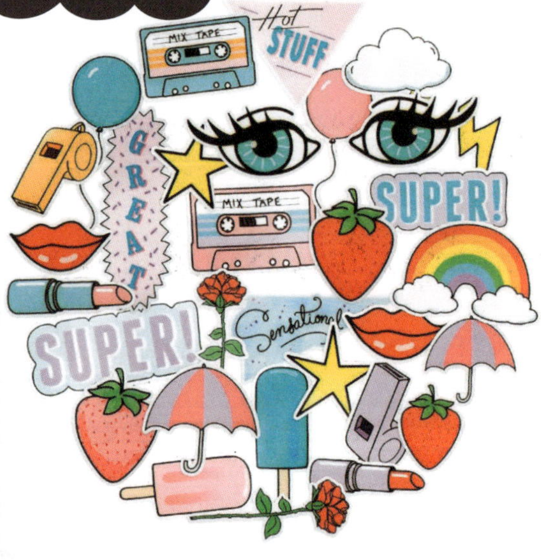

motivational
sticker style

MANTRA MOOD BOARD

VERSION 1: MANTRA FOR INSPIRATION

For the inspirational version of this mantra illustration, we'll be using shooting stars as our illustration motif. In contrast with the calming mantra artwork, the lettering here will be a much bigger feature to boost the inspiring mood and message of the piece.

The colour palette for this artwork includes bold and saturated colours intended to be eye-catching and inspiring for the viewer.

As I want the lettering to be the most prominent feature of this artwork, I'm going to be drawing a range of medium to small stars to helps emphasize the text, and give the piece movement. I also want to draw them with as little detail as possible so that the lettering stays clear to read.

I'll be using two different lettering styles here to add some more interest to the artwork, and I'm going to pick out 'progress' and 'perfection', placing them in a more eye-catching style to ensure they're the main focus. To contrast with this, the word 'not' will be written in a much simpler lettering style.

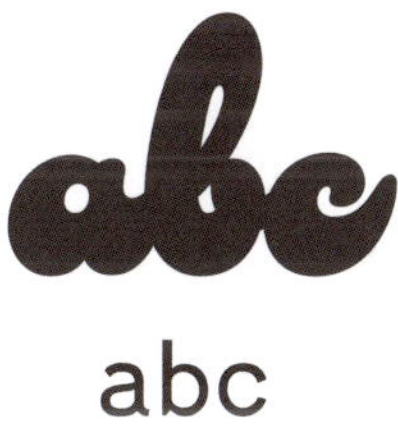

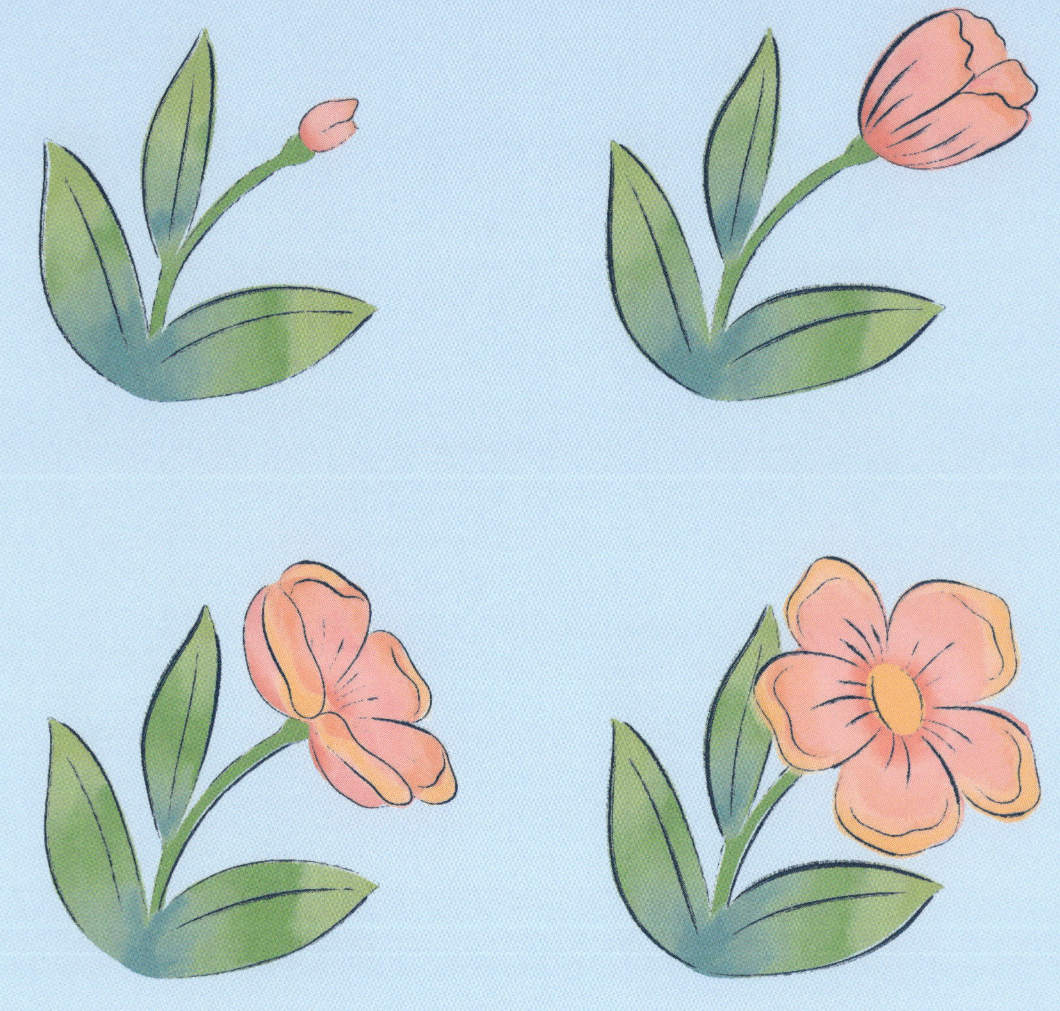

progress not
perfection

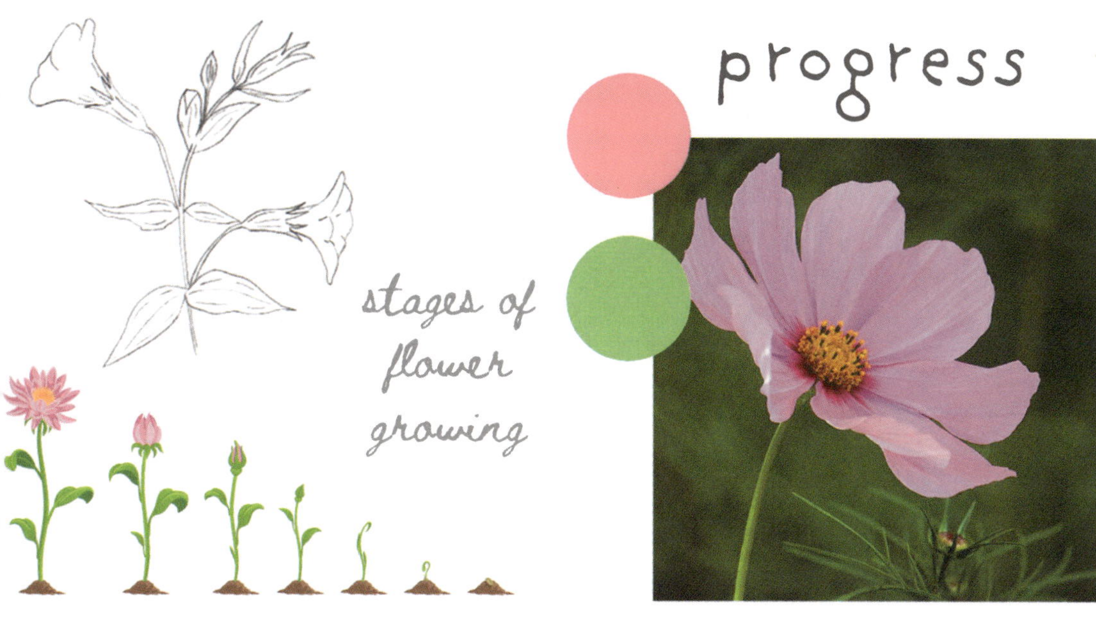

MANTRA MOOD BOARD

VERSION 2: MANTRA FOR CALMING

For the calming version of this mantra illustration, we are going to be depicting a growing flower. As this mantra is for relaxation, our illustrations are going to have a looser and more freehand feel to them, which will give the flowers an imperfect feel and appearance, further visually complementing the meaning of our mantra.

In this artwork, I have chosen to use pink and blue, as these colours will evoke feelings of calm from the viewer.

I'll be using a delicate style of drawing and writing in this piece, so the type of flower used for inspiration is important. I've chosen a cosmos, as the fragile petals and stem of this flower will create that feeling of gentleness in this artwork.

As with the illustration elements, I want to use a freehand lowercase lettering here to tie in with the 'imperfect' feel of the artwork.

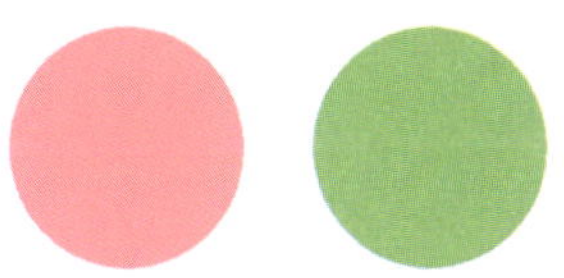

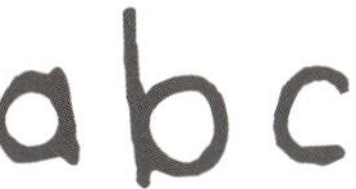

USING THE SAME MANTRA TO EVOKE DIFFERENT EMOTIONS

For this final project, I wanted to show you how you can use the different skills and techniques I have taught you to evoke different emotions, and to challenge you to make two pieces out of one mantra. Let's compare the different features of these two illustrations, and discuss the choices made for each piece, and why they are suitable. You may like to take a piece of paper to plan out and compare the unique elements that you want to use for your two mantras, and consider what you can do to make them different.

	Calming Mantra	Inspiring Mantra
Colour Palette	Light shades with a pale blue background create a tranquil atmosphere.	Bold and saturated colours are utilized here, with a darker blue background to create a more eye-catching artwork.
Lettering	A hand-drawn style of lowercase lettering is used here to convey this mantra message in a subtle way.	Two different fonts have been used here; a bold and embellished style of lettering for 'PROGRESS' and 'PERFECTION', and a simpler font written in capital letters for 'NOT', to create a striking artwork.
Elements	A dainty flower drawn in a more realistic style so the delicate process of the flower opening is clear to the viewer. This helps to create a sense of calm and balance with this piece, and the drawing has been created in a style that complements the lettering style.	Two shooting stars and smaller stars around the lettering on a night sky background drawn in a more abstracted style. In this artwork, the mantra message is the main feature and the illustrative motifs are more of a background; not using outlines and keeping the colours flat helps to not distract the eye from the message.

You can also use this additional table for inspiration and ideas when planning your own mantra projects in the future. Here, I have provided references to techniques you have learnt in this book that you may like to use to evoke these two different moods.

	Calming Mantra	Inspiring Mantra
Colour Palette	☆ Sunset colours (see page 93) ☆ Light pastel colours (see page 59)	☆ One colour (see pages 134–35) ☆ Pop Art inspired colours (see page 102) ☆ Retro inspired colours (see page 101)
Lettering	☆ Calligraphy (see pages 118–119) ☆ Lowercase lettering (see page 143) ☆ Handwritten lettering (see pages 59, 66, 143)	☆ All capital lettering (see page 77) ☆ Bold lettering (see page 133)
Elements	☆ Natural elements (see pages 38–43) ☆ Watercolour washes (see pages 60–61) ☆ Gradients (see pages 68–69)	☆ Storytelling grids (see pages 94–95) ☆ Symmetry (see page 52–53) ☆ Abstract artwork (see page 103)

COMPOSITION

VERSION 1: MANTRA FOR INSPIRATION

To create my mantra, I used Photoshop, following the steps on pages 16–23 to prepare for my project. The practical media alternative for this artwork would be coloured markers, or you could use acrylic paint for the base colours and a black pen for your writing.

BACKGROUND

I set my background colour (using the steps on page 17) to a dark blue colour to evoke the night sky. Its shade needed to be dark, but not too dark to allow our mantra message to be read.

If you are using a practical medium, paint your background colour and allow it to dry before moving on to your elements.

ELEMENTS

To start off this mantra artwork, I blocked out the colours for the rays of the shooting star and the blue background (see page 126). Next, I added in the stars for the shooting stars and around the edge.

If you are using a practical medium, you can use a pencil to mark out where you want your stars and rays to be, and then colour them in one layer at a time.

TEXT

In this artwork, the mantra message is the main focus. As there are a lot of colours in the background, I wanted the lettering to be large enough to stand out against this, while still feeling like both aspects work together overall. This is also a great opportunity to use a more decorative font.

The lettering is central, and the word 'PERFECTION' is the same width across the page as the illustrative elements in the background, to ensure it stands out while still feeling balanced.

You can easily experiment with the sizing of your lettering by using the selection tool in Photoshop, clicking on your text, and clicking and dragging on the corner of the selection box.

If you are creating this artwork using a practical medium, I would suggest adding your text using black acrylic or marker pens.

For the words 'PROGRESS' and 'PERFECTION' you could use a thicker pen to write, or if you don't have one thick enough, you could draw the outline of your letters first and colour them in. For the 'NOT', use a thinner pen to create the contrast between the two lettering styles.

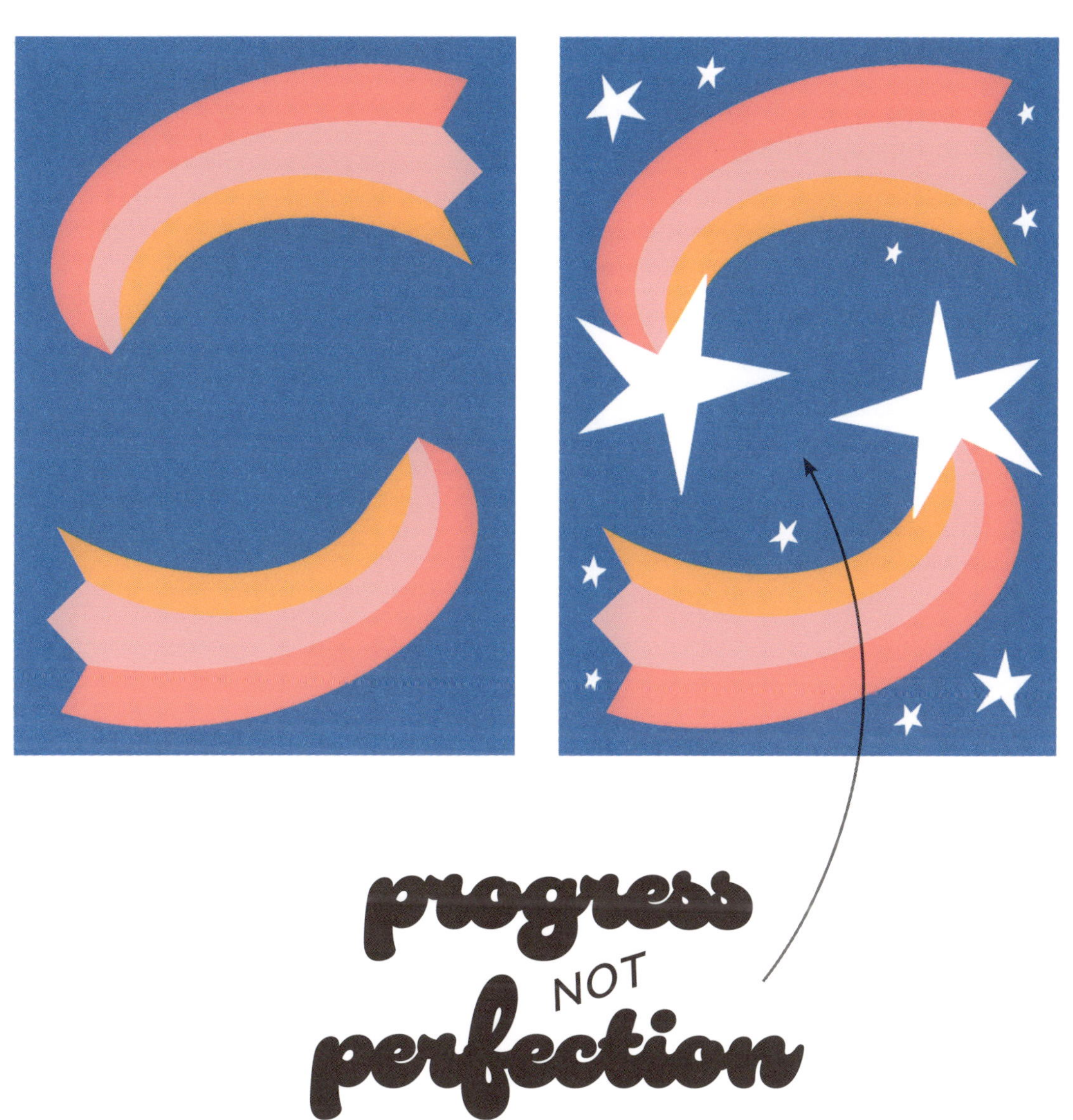

progress
NOT
perfection

COMPOSITION

VERSION 2: MANTRA FOR CALMING

To create my mantra, I used Photoshop, following the steps on pages 16–23 to prepare for my project. The practical media alternative for this artwork would be would be coloured pencil, or a mixed media approach of watercolour paint for the colour on the flowers, and pencil for the outlines and text.

ELEMENTS

I began this illustration by blocking out the colours of the flower (see page 126), before adding more details to the flowers using shadows and highlights. Once the colours were done, I used a pencil to add a light outline to the flowers and add some definition.

If using a practical medium, you can also use the steps on page 127 to help you colour block and add detail to your flowers.

TEXT

I used the font 'Providence Sans Pro'. Its simple and handwritten style works well to complement the looser drawing style used in our illustration. I didn't want the lettering to overwhelm the illustration, so the sizing and placement was important, and I experimented with the correct sizing using the steps on pages 28–29. I placed the lettering beneath the illustrations to ensure the piece remained calm and delicate.

If you are writing the lettering by hand, lowercase lettering would be the substitution for the typed font used in the example artwork.

1.
2.
3.
4.
progress not perfection

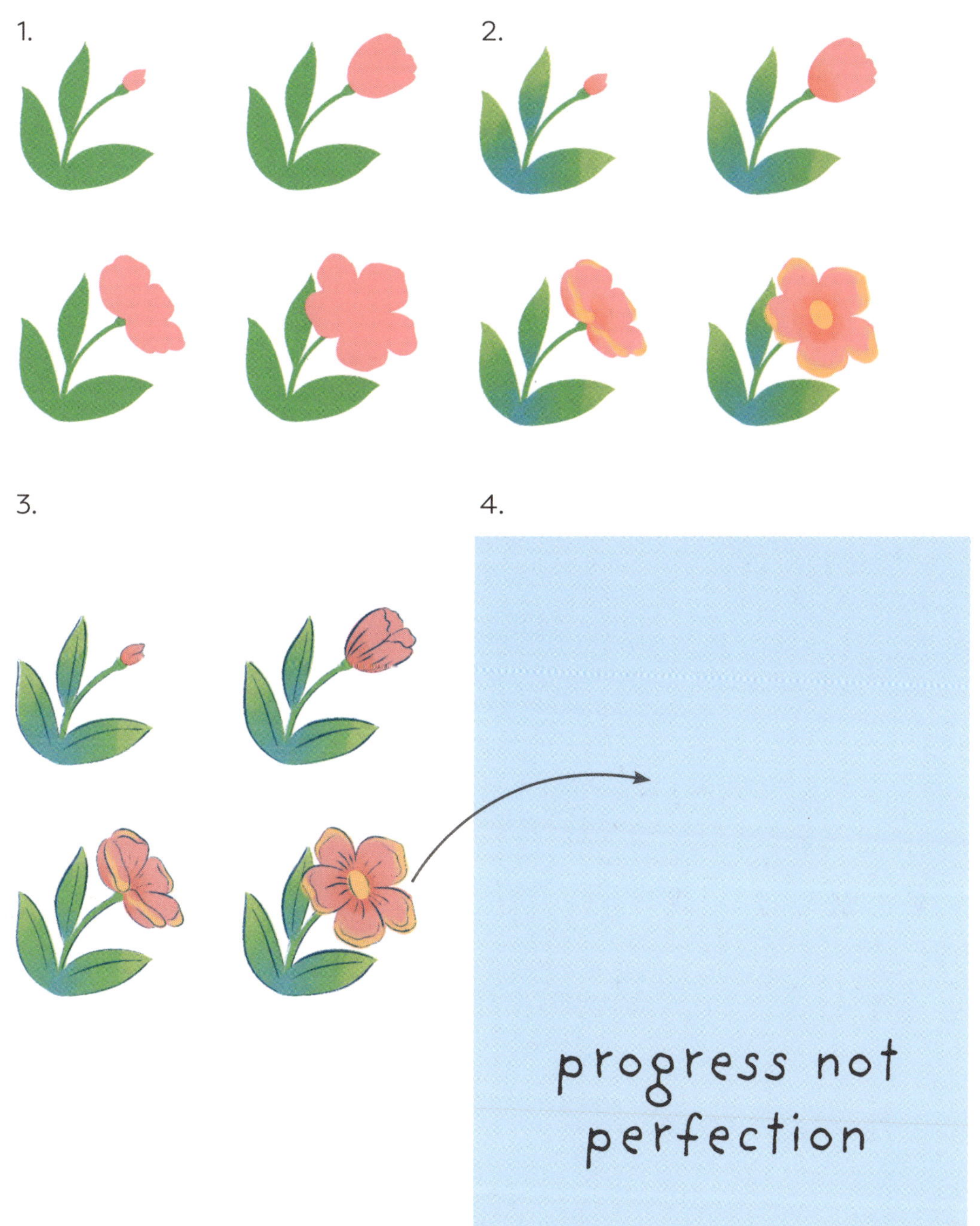

FURTHER MANTRAS FOR YOUR PROJECTS

As this book draws to a close, I hope you will continue to develop your own mantra projects inspired by everything you've learnt here. To help you carry on your mantra journey, here is a list of mantras that you can use to help inspire your pieces.

1. KEEP GROWING

2. ONE DAY AT A TIME

3. BREATHE

4. LET THINGS FLOW

5. TRUST THE PROCESS

6. DREAM BIG

7. EVERYTHING I NEED IS WITHIN ME

8. IT'S NEVER TOO LATE

9. EVERYTHING WILL BE OKAY

10. CHOOSE LOVE

11. PERSISTENCE IS KEY

12. MINDSET IS EVERYTHING

13. I CAN DO ANYTHING, BUT NOT EVERYTHING

14. DISCOMFORT MEANS GROWTH

15. I EMBRACE THE UNKNOWN

16. I AM GRATEFUL

17. I DESERVE HAPPINESS

18. I AM ENOUGH

19. TODAY IS A NEW DAY

20. DO MORE OF WHAT MAKES YOU HAPPY

CONCLUSION

I hope that the drawing projects in this book,
plus the skills you learn and develop along
the way, will be a resource you can turn
to when you want to feel calm, uplifted
or inspired!

For me, drawing has always been something
I do to relax and de-stress. It may not solve
any problems, but it helps me to create a
peaceful environment that puts me in a more
positive mindset. I hope that the projects in
this book will do the same for you, and that
you can use the skills you learn to continue
on your creative journey.

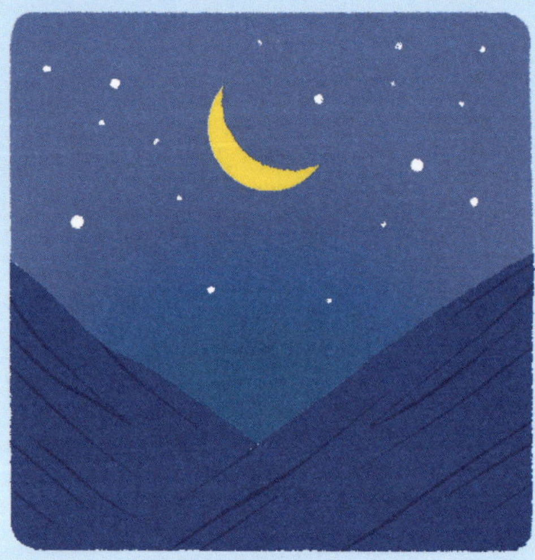

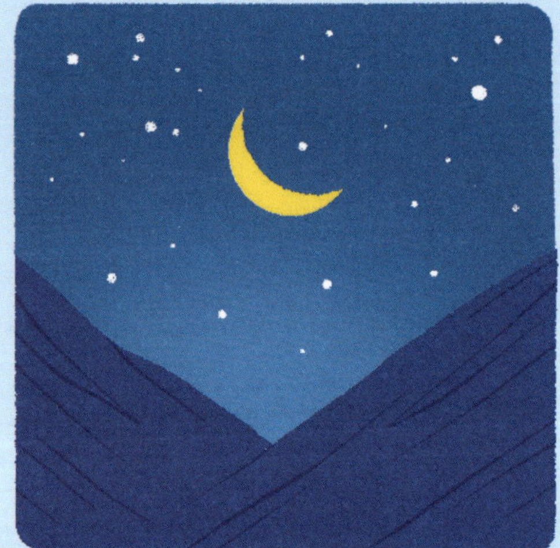

FURTHER READING

Find Your Artistic Voice: The Essential Guide to Working Your Creative Magic, by Lisa Congden, Chronicle Books, 2019.

The Art of Noticing: Rediscover What Really Matters to You, by Rob Walker, Ebury Press, 2019.

Painting Calm: Connect to nature through the art of watercolour, by Inga Buividavice, Leaping Hare Press, 2023.

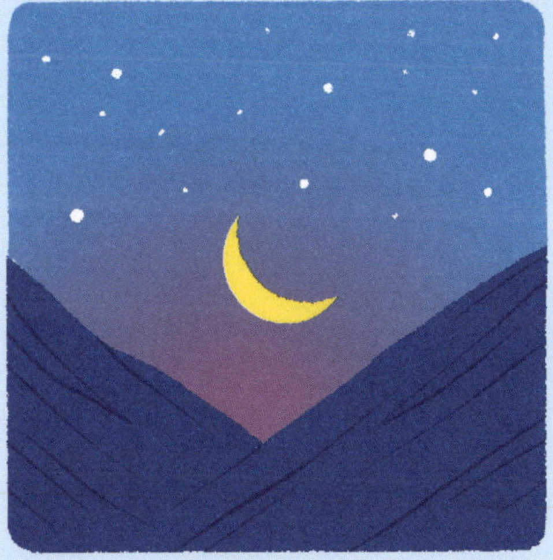

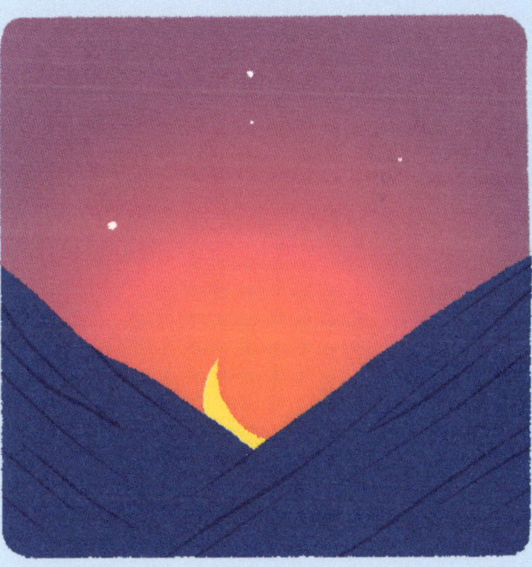

INDEX

ABOUT THE AUTHOR

Phe Johnson has been working as an illustrator since 2019. Her illustration style is heavily inspired by '90s/early '00s nostalgia, and the illustration and design styles she connected with growing up. The inspiration for her drawings comes from the appreciation of the small moments of joy that help relieve the stresses of everyday life, using a combination of bright colours, simplified and abstracted shapes, and positive quotes. She hopes that these influences will create illustrations that can become small moments of joy for others. She is the illustrator of *Cosmic Self-care*.

Instagram: **@phejohnson**

Website: **www.phejohnson.com**

Etsy: **www.etsy.com/uk/shop/ phejohnsonmakes**

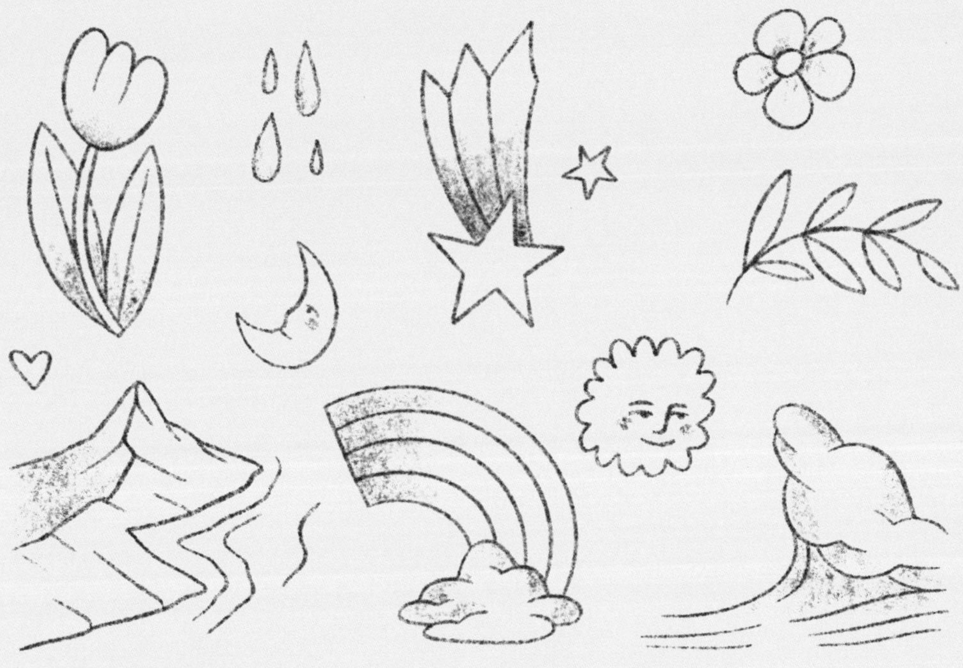

ACKNOWLEDGEMENTS

I would like to thank the team at Leaping Hare for supporting me through this project, to Monica Perdoni for reaching out to me and Chloe Murphy for guiding me through every step of the process.

Thank you to everyone who made it possible for me to get to work on this project, to my parents for always encouraging my creativity, and to my husband Conor for being a constant champion.

Thank you also to my Instagram community, for your continued support and encouragement, and for allowing my work to be seen.

PICTURE CREDITS

p.35 © Raisa Zwart, © Martin Podt, © Yulia Maslevich; p.58 © Alexa Patterson, courtesy of Freepik, © Brighten, © Mandy Disher; p.78 © WildFlowersProvence.fr, © Hampshire Historica, © Shutterstock/Predyathon R, © Vecteezy.com; p.84 © Smitha Katti, courtesy of Freepix, © Elly Russell/Alamy; © Webneel.com, courtesy of Freepik, © Shutterstock/Brian Donovan, © Vectorstock, © Vecteezy.com; p.100 © Adobestock/Mar_mite_, © Shutterstock/54613; p.108 © Adobestock/Linda, © Vecteezy.com, courtesy of Freepik, © Pexels/coldbeer; p.116 © Vecteezy.com, © Kate Petlenko; p.124 © Pixabay/Hishametto, © Gaurav Editz © DV Design; p.132 © Depositphotos.com/Zeferli, © DrGrabowskiLab; p.140 © Good Vibes 11:11, © Vecteezy.com, © Navy Peony, © John Morfis/HelloArtsy; p.143 © Getty/Rustemgurler, © Rosemary Calvert/Fine Art America, © Kerry Godsall.

Quarto

First published in 2025 by Leaping Hare Press
an imprint of The Quarto Group.

1 Triptych Place 2nd Floor,
185 Park Street, London,
United Kingdom
SE1 9SH
T (0)2077 009 000
www.Quarto.com

EEA Representation, WTS Tax d.o.o.,
Žanova ulica 3, 4000 Kranj, Slovenia

© 2025 Quarto PLC

All rights reserved. No part of this book may be reproduced or
utilized in any form or by any means, electronic or mechanical,
including photocopying, recording, or by any information
storage and retrieval system, without permission in writing from
Leaping Hare Press.

Every effort has been made to trace the copyright holders of
material quoted in this book. If application is made in writing to
the publisher, any omissions will be included in future editions.

ISBN 978-0-7112-9690-9
Ebook ISBN 978-0-7112-9691-6

10 9 8 7 6 5 4 3 2 1

Design by Hanri van Wyk
Editorial by Chloe Murphy

Printed in China